clouds over Mykonos

ISBN 960 226 346 6

Athens 1992

Printed and bound in Greece by
EFSTATHIADIS GROUP S.A.

Distributed by
EFSTATHIADIS GROUP S.A.
HEAD OFFICE: AGIOU ATHANASIOU ST. GR - 145 65 ANIXI ATTIKIS
TEL: (01) 8140602, 8140702 FAX: (01) 8142915 TELEX: 216176 EF
ATHENS BRANCH: 14 VALTETSIOU ST. GR - 106 80 ATHENS
TEL: (01) 3633319, 3614312, 3637284 FAX: (01) 3614312
ATHENS BOOKSHOP: 84 ACADEMIAS ST. TEL: 3637439
THESSALONIKI BRANCH: 4 C. CRISTALLI ST. ANTIGONIDON SQUARE
THESSALONIKI, GR - 546 30 TEL: (031) 511781, 542498, FAX 544759
THESSALONIKI BOOKSHOP: 14 ETHNIKIS AMINIS ST. TEL: (031) 278158

clouds over Mykonos

ZACHOS CHADJIFOTIOU

EFSTATHIADIS GROUP

CHAPTER 1

The sky over the Acropolis had taken on that pinkish-violet colour that every Athenian claims to be unique to Attican sunsets. It was early evening and soon the tourists would be flocking up the sacred hill to watch the "Sound and Light" performance, hardly aware that in the bushes and under the trees around them - let alone in the parked cars - couples were enjoying something more ancient than the Parthenon.

I was at Alexis' house, sitting alone on the small terrace that overlooked the Acropolis. The magnificent view and the prominently displayed old photograph of Alexis' father when he was Minister of Finance were the only remembrances of a glorious past which Alexis tried to revive by throwing parties for his childhood friends every so often. How often, depended on when he could afford to hire waiters from the Grande Bretagne, Athens' most exclusive hotel for over a century. Alexis would settle for no less; they were the only waiters in town who could be distinguished from those employed at lower-class establishments by the blue line edging their crisp white jackets, and Alexis knew that his guests appreciated such details.

Poor Alexis, who could hardly put aside enough money to pay the rent, used whatever was left of his resources to create a semblance of the old family mansion in his crowded new quarters. The massive furniture looked like hand-me-downs in the small rooms of the rented apartment; its low ceilings seemed to be supported by the enormous bookcases, but Alexis wouldn't think of parting with them when he was forced to sell the stately old house and most of its furnishings.

Alexis' guests list was another of his most prized possessions; the names had barely changed over the decades that we've known one another. I often wondered why he still invited me to his parties. As I stepped back into the room to refill my glass, I looked over the old crowd and wondered whether I was the only one who had changed, or if I had been different from the start.

Their values remained the same as thirty years ago, when the supreme ambition in life was to be accepted by the Tennis Club. We had all applied at the same time, and most of us had been accepted. It had been such a closed circle in the old days, that it took the older members two years before tthey deigned to look our way. They used to refer to us as "the repairmen", - not because we were in that business, but because this symbol of power and wealth was desperately in need of money for repairs after the German occupation, which had left the members with their great names but very little cash. After much hesitation, they decided to raise it by accepting carefully chosen new members.

I smiled to myself as I remembered one particularly ambitious fellow who carried on an affair with an elderly member for two whole years before she put in a good word for him with the board of directors.

Amusing myself with such memories, I thought of how the people in this room resembled a yellowed old photograph hanging on a crumbling wall, when I suddenly noticed a face that didn't belong in the photograph. She must have been twenty years younger than everyone else - certainly not more than thirty. She was pretty in a way unusual for a Greek girl: small and fragile, with an intelligent, pixie-like face. She came smiling towards me:

"You know, ten years ago I was in love with you!" she announced.

I tried to place her somewhere in my tumultuous past but couldn't, so without thinking I answered "Luckily you got over it" and walked away.

CHAPTER 2

A few days later my doorbell rang at eight in the morning - a very unusual hour for my doorbell, which usually wakes up with me at about eleven.

It was a woman carrying a book:

"Miss Papazisi sends this for you", she said.

Not fully awake, I dropped the book on a table and went back to sleep. Two hours later I was having coffee with the book in my hand. When I read the dedication I realized who Miss Papazisi was: "For you, Marilena", it said:

"Well," I thought to myself, lighting the day's first cigarette, the pixie face at Alexis' is a writer!"

The book was entitled "The ex-communicated." I started reading it at three and by nine I was finished. It was a very good book, and I found her telephone number to tell her so. She was out.

The next day I called her again. I had to thank her, even though I'm usually not all that polite. Of course, I could have sent her a thank you note, but I felt I had to do it personally. She picked the phone up herself:

"Did you like it?" she asked right away.

"Very much," I answered plainly, knowing it meant more than a thousand thank-you's.

"I'd like to ask you a few things about it;", I went on.

"Gladly, but I don't think it can be done over the

phone."

That night we dined at "Heaven's Garden" in the Plaka district. She was a good talker. She was a clear thinker. She wasn't a drinker, and that wasn't good. I like people who drink; they liberate themselves and they stop racking their brain before opening their mouths.

We ended up at my place. I was asleep when she left. I didn't hear from her again, until my doorbell rang again a few days later. It was the same woman who had delivered the book. This time she was carrying a letter. The strange new girl in my life acted as if there was no telephone, no mail service. Victor Hugo's "Letters of Love" came to my mind I tore open the letter and read:

My dear Don,

For months, if not for a year, my pen rested on my tidy desk, like the whore who goes to a convent for atonement.

But suddenly, you've excited it. You've provoked it, and it's started once more to keep company with my imagination.

Many times in the past, except in moments of true inspiration, I wrote only so I could put down on paper a little of my loneliness or to kill time before it engulfed me with its vulgar stillness. Sometimes I wrote simply because it was the only thing I know how to do no matter if I do it well or badly.

Being a colleague, you must also have felt that a writer, whether great or mediocre, famous or ignored, is a version of god, since it is he who creates his heroes, entagles them in adventures, makes them fall in love according to his wishes, emburdens them with problems simply because he himself has problems and throws them into the jungle called life at will.

11

Francois Sagan wrote: "Wordliness stabs even our vices", and I isolated the phrase from the rest of the text because it struck home.

Fate must have been in a good mood the night she threw us together, like garbage in an expensive garbage can. Among the others, you and I were like day and night. And yet, think that they come and part twice every twentyfour hours, while it took us almost three decades to meet!

What were we doing there. You, I imagine, came out of habit because you have no vices, as far as I know; whereas I came to stab my vice - if I may use the phrase - the vice of still insisting on looking for people rather than animals that act like people.

As I was sitting there listening to nonsense spoken in a faked french accent, I noticed you and thought of a phrase from dostoyefsky: "Even if there is no god, we should invent one." But as I was looking in vain for my hero, watching you play the role of a bored don juan, I said to myself: "Even if this man isn't the don quixote I'm looking for, I must invent him."

And so I decided to create you.

The other day at your place, you made me laugh as I hadn't in years - not that I'm miserable. "Nothing is more ridiculous than misery", Becket wrote and he managed to affect me. The one thing I fear is the ridiculous.

To get back to that night, I don't remember how many hours we spent together.

I remember, though, that I had a plan in mind when I came to you - to watch you, to spy on you, to analyze you - but I forgot it and I let myself be carried away into your world, the world of the man I imagined you were.

My dear don, we learn nothing from the people who

love us. "Fall in love and become stupid", Pascal said. So let me teach you something about yourself, since I'm not in love with you - at least not yet - and haven't become stupid.

You and yourself, I and my imagination, will look at Stratis in four dimension.

A bit of advice, before I forget: Don't be angry with people whose faults annoy you - you owe them the knowledge of what bothers you. If it weren't for them, would you know, for instance, that pompousness annoyes you? You have something to learn from everyone, even if you pay for it. Honest people always pay their bills.

So, I was bringing to mind and reliving our moments together, mixed up like shreds of charm.

A few words here and there, your past loves - here the laughing Don Juan appeared - and suddenly you spoke of her ... the great adventure you would embark on, if you could. And then I saw you, thin and wrinkled, sad, romantic, turning into Don Quixote riding a tired old horse.

That didn't last long, either. You threw off your rusty armor, took on your protective look and warned me of a danger threatening me, the danger of falling in love with you. You know that I'm running no such danger, but subconsciously perhaps you want me to. I can assure you, on the other hand, that I'd like it very much, if I still can.

So who are you, I wondered while lighting yet another cigarette, lying in bed and staring at a moon that was hidden by clouds Don Juan or Don quixote?

My doubts lasted as long as it took the cigarette to burn my fingers and my eyes to close from the blinding light of the hidden moon. I fell asleep and dreamed a crazy, faceless dream: colourful, willowy, elegant and bright shadows mixed in with grayish, melancholy ones. I woke up. Not being froyd, I interpreted it like a bad student of his. The problem on my mind unwound itself like a spool of thread: You're both heroes together, Don Juan and Don Quixote wrapped into one. Colourful trousers worn with a dark jacket.

And just as the answer came to me, I made yet another realization: the two characters are blood relations. One lived; the other imagined that he lived. One charmed; the other was charmed. That's about it for now. Perhaps if we should meet again, I'll tell you more of my secrets. The secrets that only I know, because I'm the one who discovered you and it makes me feel like a miniature columbus.

If, by chance, you find the things I wrote figments of my imagination, remember that America didn't know who she was either, until columbus discovered her one Tuesday in November .... (the year escapes me).

"Marilena

When I put down the letter, I had already started answering to the name don. The girl definitely had something. Without wanting to admit it, I agreed that she was a little columbus. She had managed in just a few hours with me to grasp a lot which, of course, I knew about myself but had never seen on paper before.

At the same time, I wondered whether she was in love with me now, rather than ten years ago. Or maybe she had gotten over the first attack and was now on the second - something like a recurring flu.

In any case, I can't imagine what got into me the next night, when I saw her again and blurted out: "Since you've never been to Mykonos, come with me and I'll show you around. I'm leaving the day after tomorrow."

CHAPTER 3

"Which island are we passing now, Don?"

"I already told you, it's Yiaros, the island that was a prison camp during the dictatorship."

"Oh, com'n, you said the same thing two hours ago. Where's your mind wandering to, don?"

"I don't know. All I know is that now I'm wandering with you towards Mykonos, and you've never been there before. That can be dangerous."

"What do you mean?" I know all about Mykonos. Everyone does", she answered. "Allright, allright. It's gotten to the point that Mykonos is better known than Greece Last year, as I was standing in line at the Olympic counter in New Year to get a return ticket to Athens, the lady in front me was asking the clerk how far Greece is from Mykonos."

"And what did the girl answer."

"She didn't. I did."

"Good God, the poor woman!."

"No, no. I didn't attack her I was very polite. I told her that attempts are being made to unite greece with mother Mykonos one day. I went on that way, telling her that when the day comes, the greek capital will be moved to Mykonos, together with the Acropolis. She found it a great idea, and added that if the vatican, too, was moved to Mykonos, it would be a great time-saver for tourists - they could squeeze in the Acropolis, the vatican and the pelican in Mykonos, that Jackie Onasis became so attached to, all in one day."

"You're terrible," Marilena laughed.

"I'm not terrible, I'm just Greek. When I'm abroad, I could kill anyone who criticizes Greece. When I'm here, I become more critical than the worst critic. Mykonos, for instance. I must be crazy taking you to Mykonos for the first time. You'll probably hate it. I don't know you. I don't know what your tastes are. If your likes are similar to most people's, you'll ruin my vacation and yours, too. You may go for tree-lined landscapes and comfort. You won't find either in Mykonos." She had opened her eyes wide, looking at me in disbelief: "how can Mykonos have nothing", she wondered "and attract half a million tourists every year?"

"That's because there are half a million lunatics in the world, and they all gather on Mykonos every year to join the other lunatics who live there."

She didn't seem to understand and I went on:

"How can I explain it baby? Normal people come to Mykonos and say, It's a lovely island, but aren't there any trees?" No, sir. There are no trees. There are fifty islands in greece, with trees and shrubs. But none in Mykonos. Or rather, there was a tree years ago. They painted it white so it would blend in with the rest of the scenery. They whitewash the streets twice a week in Mykonos. You think they would let a tree stay green?"

Now I realized my mistake in taking Marilena with me. What was she going to do? She had a strange, patient look on her face and her patience tended to neutralize my hot-headedness.

She tolerated a lot from me, and all of it with a good-

The book's story full of human passion, love and many clouds, unfolds in this magical atmosphere

Paraportiani". This church was not made by human hand, but by God himself along with the clouds and light that surround it.

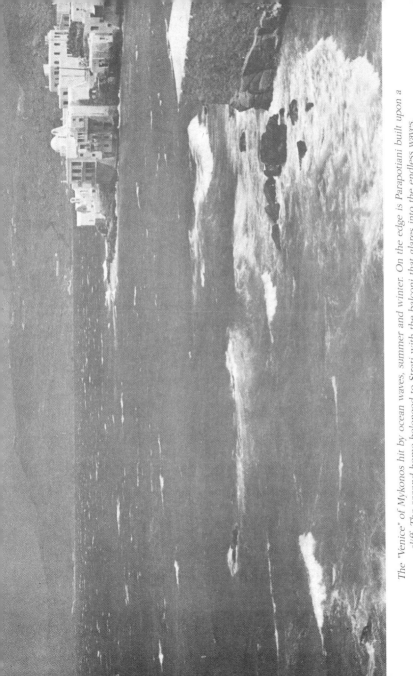

The "Venice" of Mykonos hit by ocean waves, summer and winter. On the edge is Parapotiani built upon a cliff. The second home belonged to Strati with the balconi that glares into the endless waves.

Paraportiani against the sun. The whitest colour on earth.

"Venice". The loveliest neighbourhood on earth, where the sound of the waves and the cheerful voices of the children, make you feel "human", but of the lucky humans.

Once you have lived in this neighbourhood, you won't be able to live anywhere else.

Everything is white in Mykonos. This tourist here that whitens the "9 Mousses" will be drinking free for a week.

Every friday compulsory street whitening. Everyone in front of their home or shop.

natured smile. Although she denied it, I'm sure she felt something for me, a small spark of love maybe.

So what? There was nothing new about that. But where was she heading? What kind of adventure was she being led into? I'm not cut out for affairs with nice girls.

"Tell me, Don," she went on, "now that you've told me about the trees that Mykonos doesn't have, can you tell me what else it doesn't have?"

"Nothing. It doesn't have anything."

"Cut it out, Don Quixote. Don't tell me Mykonos doesn't have a subway system. I don't expect it to."

"Who's talking about subways? I'm talking about water. Clear, simple drinking water. Mykonos doesn't have any."

"What?" she asked, shocked.

"Yes, love, Mykonos has no water. And when I say water, I don't mean niagara falls. I mean water to drink and wash with."

She looked at me wide-eyed again, unable to believe it.

"Well, let's not exagerate?" I calmed her. "When, the weather allows it the boat comes in from Athens, and there is plenty of drinking water. The bottled variety, at four drachmas per bottle. No, I'm sorry. Milk goes for four drachmas. Water costs six. And, in addition to being great for the digestive system, bottled water is perfect for a shower. with three bottles - eighteen drachmas - you can wash off all the sea salt on your body. In any case, what is known as a water supply, doesn't exist in Mykonos.

She went on looking at me, laughing and not believing a word, while I told her about the faucets that usually blurt out air - very refreshing on a hot summer day. Now that I had filled I felt less guilty in on the situation, about all the things Mykonos couldn't offer the civilized world. Anyhow, I thought, it was only an island - it wasn't my house. All I had said was "I'm going to Mykonos. Want to come along?" And since that night, she lived with that dream, went to sleep with it at night and woke up with it the next morning.

We were on our way! ...

CHAPTER 4

"The boat is rocking, don"

"The boat always rocks when we're approaching."

"Why does it do that, don?"

"Because it's windy."

"Oh, and I hate the wind!."

At this point I ordered a double scotch and gulped it down, speechless. "Why aren't you talking to me, don?"

I swallowed the last drop and asked her again, just in case I hadn't heard well:

"Are you sure you don't like the wind."

"yes, why? Is it that terrible?"

"It's not terrible, it's a tragedy if you're going to Mykonos and you don't like the wind."

"I don't understand."

"It's windy in Mykonos, baby. It's very windy."

"I still don't understand", she said, obviously upset.

"Look, darling, I went on softly, because I had been too abrupt on her and she was getting scared.

"Mykonos is an island like all other islands. It has a north and a south side. On the north side, it's windy. It's windy all the time. On the south side, it's calm and lovely. Unfortunately, everything happens on the north side of Mykonos. The city is built on the north, the harbor is on the north, the boats anchor on the north and everyone lives on the north.

"In Mykonos", I continued, "We know how many beauforts there are by what the wind carries away. When only the chairs of the sidewalk cafes are turned over, we called it a chair wind that means 7 beauforts. When it carries away the tables, too, we call it a "table wind." That means 8.5 beauforts. When the churchbells start ringing ..."

"I know", she cut in, "it's a catastrophe." Her eyes had a look of wonder and fear in them, but also one of childish joy. I don't understand why people built the city on the side of the catastrophes", the insisted.

"You can't understand. And you shouldn't ask why this and why that about Mykonos. The people of Mykonos are and always were crazy. The wind drives you crazy, or didn't you know?"

"Then, what about the beautiful sea and the golden beaches that everyone talks about."

"I already told you, they're on the south side.

"And how far is the south side."

"Seven kilometers, I answered, and she seemed comforted by that. Good, so we can go to the south to swim. Seven kilometers isn't all that much.

"By car, no, it isn't" I answered.

"Why do you say that? I didn't ask you to walk there, did I?"

"You didn't ask me to, but that's probably the way it'll be."

"Oh, com'n. Stop putting me on. Now you'll tell me there are no cars." She kidded.

How could I explain? I ordered another double scotch, I sipped some, took a deep breath and started to explain patiently.

"Listen, Marilena, I didn't say there aren't any cars ...

20

Then it is simple, she interrupted. "It's simple, love, only if you go on foot. But seven plus seven kilometers back makes for fourteen, and that's no joke in the scorching sun. But certainly it's not any case to go by car. There are nine taxis on the island and at least - no exggeration - nine thousand people who want to go to the beach between ten and twelve. With a little simple arithmetic, you'll see that it's impossible to transports these people in twenty two hours, let alone two!"

"So who are the lucky ones who get to the beach, you're probably wondering. Certainly no one gets in to the cars by chance. In Mykonos, there's a class structure, tradition and respect for both. So, the first to get in the cabs are the godfathers of the drivers' children. I've christened the children of all nine, so I'm no problem second in line are the village doctor, the priest and the mayor. Third, the descendants of the local heroes in the war of independence against the turks. Fourth, come Fouskis, Billy, Apostolis and Kyriakos."

"Who are they?" she wanted to know.

I tried to explain that they're the island's "tough guys", but she couldn't get it through her head.

"What I mean is, that they've formed a gang and they do as they please anywhere on the island. It's a matter of life and death for the driver. Now do you understand?" "I understand, but I'm getting scared with all the things you're saying.

"There's no reason to be afraid of those four."

"And why not?"

"Because, in a way, I'm their spiritual father."

"Well, long live your fine children! go on, now, with the seniority list. I'm anxious to see when it'll be my turn to get into the cab."

"You have no problem, love. You have rights in two categories - the first and the last - so you'll be in the first cab for sure."

"Anyhow, I'm curious. Go on ..."

"Well, afterwards, Antonis who is deaf and dumb gets in. The reason is simple: He's deaf and so doesn't hear the others yelling at him. Then Lambros, the policeman gets in. That's because he's on duty. His duty is to arrest the nudists before they have time to put their clothes on."

"You mean that such things happen in Mykonos?"

"What do you mean by such things?" The nudism or the affected morality?"

"I mean the affected morality."

"You must be joking. Mykonos is without a doubt the most modest Island in Greece. Everyone imagines Mykonos as the "Whore of the Aegean." I assure you that "the virgin of the aegean" would be more appropriate? The law is present everywhere. Enforcement officers are even ready to wipe out any punishable act, any violation of the law, any act that upsets the peace and quiet of the Island, any abnormality, even if it is sexual, because ..."

"Oh, cut it out", she burst out laughing.

CHAPTER 5

"Attention! Attention!" the loudspeakers announced. Would all passengers for Mykonos please prepare to disembark. The ship will be docking in ten minutes."

"Well, what do you know!" I remarked.

"What's the matter this time?" Marilena snapped.

"Nothing, nothing. I was amused by the use of the verb "to dock." "Well, what did you expect him to say? We're arriving, aren't we?"

"He could say simply that we're arriving."

"I don't understand again."

"You'll understand in a minute what "to dock" in Mykonos means ..."

Meanwhile we were on line to pick up our luggage. I could hear the anchors dropping and couldn't help a secret smile as I thought of Marilena's reaction when she saw where we'd docked.

I didn't wait long. We were approaching the exit when her jaw dropped open as she saw the harbor at least a mile and a half away.

"Aren't we going any further?" she asked timidly.

"You heard what the man said: We've docked!"

"And how ... how will we get to the harbor?"

The boat was surrounded by enormous white waves while the little caiques that would take us to shore were making heroic efforts to reach us. Marilena was enraged when she saw the sarcastic smile on my face.

"Just because you're a callous beast and don't mind coming here even in winter, doesn't mean the rest of us should volunteer to drown!"

"Don't exaggerate, for Pete's sake! You think people drown so easily?"

I had to calm her down now; she may have wanted to turn back, the way she had worked herself up. The other first-timers weren't reacting any better. Already a plump, middle-aged woman was screaming in terror:

"I'm not getting into that thing! Never! The heck with Mykonos!" she yelled at her husband.

"Calm down, dear," he tried to soothe her, those "things" have been transporting people for years and no one's over drowned."

"No, No!" I can't do it! Look at the way the waves cover them!"

"Yes, dear, but they come out again!"

"And what if they don't!"

The poor man was losing his patience, while I realized that this hysterical woman was beginning to affect the other passengers. "See what the woman is saying?" Marilena cried.

I had no choice but to take drastic measures at this point.

"Listen lady, either get in the boat or else go back to your cabin and return to Piraeus."

Her husband, who under other circumstances wouldn't let anyone talk to his wife that way, readily agreed with me:

"That's right, mister, tell her she's acting silly."

"We're not going to start a conversation now. Take your wife and put her on the boat!"

My tone must have revealed the rage I felt, and like obedient children they both picked up their suitcases and went down the steps. The funny thing was that Marilena, too, stopped complaining and followed them.

But the decision to get off the big boat and into the little one was only the first step. The problem now, was how to do it. The caique underneath rocked up and down; as soon as our plump friend tried to step into it, the caique swept down again and she was left hanging there, once more hysterical.

The boatsman was used to such sights, and as he was loading the luggage onto his boat, he picked her up like another suitcase and threw her in. Now her husband was trying to get in, while she went on screaming for someone to help him until he finally made it.

Marilena and I followed quietly. The little boat was filling up.

CHAPTER 6

Marilena and I were sitting in the back of the caique.

She was obviously a bit upset as she watched more and more people cramming into the little boat, but she was trying to be brave and didn't show it. Meanwhile I was watching Mrs. Soula - by now everyone knew her name - whose face was distorted in agony. Finally she couldn't stand it any more and screamed at the boatsman:

"That's enough! We're going to drown if you pack more people in here!"

That was hardly the thing to say with forty people packed like sardines in a wildly swaying boat, so since he couldn't throw her into the sea, he decided to take no more passengers. We took off.

During the ten-minute ride Mrs. Soula rhythmically accompanied the boat's movements with "Oh's" for the ups and "Ah's" for the downs.

The least I expected her to do when we finally docked - for real this time - was to kneel down and kiss the earth. But once more the female sex disappointed me: She simply straightened out her pantsuit, ran a comb through her hair and haughtily walked off, while her husband followed with the luggage.

Marilena, too, surprised me. Instead of being annoyed by the raging wind, she had a look of ecstasy on her face as it pushed her hair backwards. She looked happy and proud as she watched my local friends rush to greet me.

I couldn't understand this strange girl, or maybe she didn't want to understand me. Not once in my life when I told a woman the truth did she believe me. Marilena was no different.

"Marilena," I had warned her before starting off for Mykonos, "I don't want you to have any false expectations that could disappoint you later."

She answered that I have another world inside me, while I live in the real one only on the surface.

"Yes, dear, but the inside world is uninhabited. There hasn't been a woman who could dwell there and I'm not looking for one.

I like to be alone. I like the independence that solitude offers. I enjoy being with the people I love only when I love them. I don't want anyone's love to claim rights on me."

She said I was an egotist; I felt like I was listening to an old recording. If she didn't believe me, it certainly wasn't my fault. My conscience was clear. She had agreed to come along - how long she would last was up to her.

We were walking along the cobblestone streets towards Apostolis' tavern. For me, it was like returning home. Every whitewashed corner, every windmill, every fishing boat was a known and beloved object. For Marilena, it was a totally new epxerience: she was looking around in childish wonder, trying to take in all the breathtaking whiteness at once.

She had wanted to see the house first, but I found the idea too domesticated for my taste. Anyhow, I was anxious to get to the tavern, where, local custom had it, my friends and I gathered on the night of my arrival to drink and laugh and eat and drink some more.

The smell of freshly-caught fish frying greeted us even before we entered the small tavern. By the door, Apostolis and his wife Theodora were waiting in welcome. Soon there were a dozen of us at the table, consuming retsina like it was water and laughing with the stories that we've laughted with for years and years, stories that each time seemed funnier.

Marilena was at my side, looking amused and happy to be there. I told her about Theodora, who drops an anchor from her window every night so the wind won't take away her little house. When the anchor was in place, she went soundly off to sleep, like a tired old captain who had finally reached land.

I liked and admired Theodora. She did as she pleased; she was her own master. But Marilena was another story. Just sitting there, smiling quietly next to me, she managed to get on my nerves. She was trying to get to my inner being, but that kind of relationship isn't for me, I felt free, uninhibited, often negative. I was tidy in my drinking, but tidiness in anything else annoyed me. I doubted she could understand that. I doubted whether anyone could. I felt at home among these islanders; I had fun in their company. I wanted to drink and laugh with them and then to break through the doors and let the wind whip me into soberness. What on earth was Marilena doing next to me? She reminded me of a thermostat that was trying to regulate my temperature. I wanted none of it.

Carried away by such thoughts and several bottles of wine, I gave the table a violent kick and it went tumbling over, plates, bottles and all.

Marilena looked at me in terror. Before she could utter a word, someone had taken her by the hand and walked her to the house.

I stepped out for a breath of air and I was my usual self when I went back in. We went on drinking until well after midnight.

CHAPTER 7

The next morning I was reading in the sitting room of the house, which is built on a platform in the sea. The windows were wide open and the sea breeze was beginning to clear my confused head.

She came up from behind and put her arms around me. She leaned and kissed my cheeck.

"How's my captain this morning?"

"So now I'm a captain, too!" I answered cheerfully - a rare condition for me in the morning. The wine must have had long-lasting effects, I mused.

Marilena made me another cup of coffee, but it was a disaster like everything else about her. She must have put at least three spoon-fuls of coffee in it and I started trembling as if I had Parkinson's disease. A dip in the sea will help me recover, I thought.

"Time for the beach," I announced, "Are you coming?"

Hurriedly she located her beach bag and we were off. As we were approaching the little square where at least a hundred people were waiting to get on a vehicle for the sea, Marilena gasped and asked meekly, "Now what?"

"What do you mean, now what?" I snapped.

"Now what are we going to do?"

I didn't answer and walked on. Suddenly a taxi appeared from around the corner and almost ran into me. It was my friend Nicolas driving and we got in before anyone had time to complain. He was ready to go when a readish-blonde head appeared at the window saying: "Hello, there. How are you? Can we come along for company?"

I didn't mind the "hello, how are you" part. I did mind the "company" part, since it was the last person on the island I wanted for company: Mrs. Soula in her pantsuit, her husband following faithfully a few steps behind.

Before I got a chance to answer they had both squeezed into the front seat, next to the driver.

"Where are these two going?" Nicolas, the driver, turned towards me, ignoring their presence next to him.

"I don't know", I answered. "We're going to Psarrou."

"What's Psarrou?" Soula's voice queried like a nightmare in the morning sunlight.

"The beach" Nicolas answered drily and thus ended the conversation.

That kept her quiet for a few minutes. She then turned to Marilena, who hadn't said a word so far.

"Did you find a place to stay, Miss?"

Nicolas answered for her:

"We have a place to stay. What about you?"

"Oh, it's terrible", Mrs Soula answered. "Just think that it was hours before we finally found a room - and some room we found!"

"Well, you were lucky" the driver continued in the same nasty tone. "Most people either sleep on the beach or return on the same boat."

At this point I cut in because Nicolas was being too abrupt, and asked her about the accommodations. I then went on to explain why most people can't find rooms on Mykonos:

"You see, my dear lady, Greece, which aspires to

became the number one tourist attraction in Europe, has over one hundred thousand hotel beds available. Even in the most remote areas, you can find a bed to sleep in. So, of these one hundred thousand, Mykonos - Greece's most famous tourist center - has a grand total of eighty-nine! Now, if you divide the three hundred thousand visitors who come to Mykonos each summer, by 89, you'll see that each one is allowed about three and a half minutes of sleep each night.

"But so what? People don't come to Mykonos to sleep - they could stay home in that case. They come here to enjoy the sun and the sea! And, in any case, there is private initiative - every summer, there's hardly a house on the island that doesn't become a little "Hilton." Also, there are the churches - 362 of them - which are used as sleeping quarters by the more religiously inclined visitors ..."

I didn't have time to hear Mrs. Soula's reactions to all this, because meantime we had reached Psarrou and Nicolas, again in his abrupt manner, opened the door and announced:

"Out, now, out. We're here!"

Mrs. Soula's mate, who had remained quiet during the entire ride, started to pay the driver. Nicolas wouldn't hear of it:

"I don't need your money, mister. Just get out!" he snapped. Unperturbed, Soula took her spouse's hand and led him out of the cab.

Mykonos only had one tree and that too was painted white one morning. It didn't fit in with the rest of the Island.

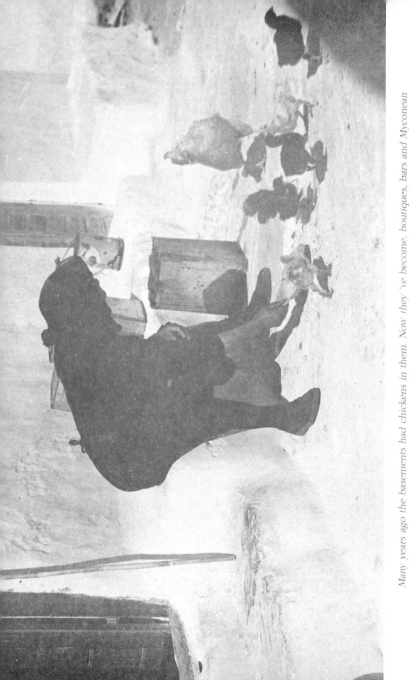

Many years ago the basements had chickens in them. Now they've become, boutiques, bars and Myconean "Hilton" type rooms.

Outside these Myconean "Hiltons" sit Tara, Anouso and Mado, waiting for their customers.

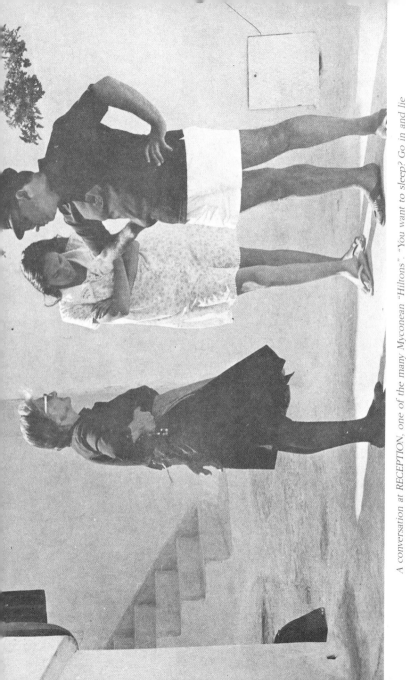

A conversation at RECEPTION: one of the many Myconean "Hiltons". "You want to sleep? Go in and lie down. You look bewitched to me".

Swimming is a real enjoyment .... but first you have to get to the beach.

The "law" vigilant and observative.

The "law" deliberates.

The "law" intervenes.

CHAPTER 8

The four of us started walking down the little hill that leads to the sandy bay known as Psarrou. There are two tavernas at Psarrou - a large one that attracts the likes of Mrs. Soula, and a small one, hidden in the reeds, that was frequented only by the island's old-timers. Marilena an,along with Nicolas, headed for the latter.

Seated on the elevated terrace, we looked over the reeds towards the beautiful bay. On either side, houses built in the simple but elegant local style were perched on the bare grey cliff. They dazzled snow-white in the brilliant mid-morning sunlight.

We were drinking our first round of ouzo and Marilena was scolding us for our treatment of Mrs. Soula:

"Whatever made you act like that? It's not the woman's fault if she's ignorant!"

"I'm sorry, sweetheart," Nicolas answered, but it's not our fault, either! Just thinking of her makes my stomach turn over!"

"That's obvious" Marilena said sarcastically. "You can't even finish your drink, poor thing: So what did she say so terrible."

"It's not what she said - it was everything about her; And that perfume."

"Yes, the perfume really was disgusting", I agreed.

"You're both unbearable" Marilena said, engared. You

stink of ouzo night and day, and the perfume bothered you!"

Just then, Calliope - owner of the taverna, cook and waitress - was bringing the second carafe of ouzo, along with tzatziki, kopanisti, and green onions. Talk of smells!

"The poor babies", Marilena went on, emboldened by the strong aromas, "The perfume made them dizzy! Why, with all the ouze in your system, you wouldn't even need an anesthetic for an operation!"

Calliope had sat down at our table and agreed heartily:

"That's right, sweetheart, tell them! And you haven't seen anything yet! Wait until you see them altogether!"

"I've seen them already" Marilena said sadly. "Last night."

Why she was sad when she spoke of something that was joy for us, I couldn't figure out. It was probably because she felt that liquor and the company of my friends deprived her of owning me exclusively, which she felt she had a right to.

"Well, now you'll see their condition even better! The sun seems to inspire them - they know they have the whole day ahead of them and so they can drink and drink and drink!"

She stood up, looked toward the sea and exclaimed:

"Here they come!"

"Here comes who?" Marilena asked uneasily.

"The pirates," Calliope explained, pointing towards a small fishing boat that was riding the waves and quickly approaching the bay.

Marilena laughed. "The bucanncers are coming on that little thing?" "Wait until you see what's in that little thing, sweetheart," Nicolas jokingly warned her. "You won't believe your eyes."

Nicolas and I knew who were coming, and I enjoyed keeping Marilena in anticipation. Although I considered her desire to own me illegal - since she had no rights on me - I thought it natural to consider her mine. My egotism imagined that she would be lost without my influence, especially in Mykonos. She certainly gave that impression. She was a very smart girl, grasping the meaning of every situation before I had time to realize it. She was dangerously smart, and that was what I liked most about her.

The little boat had landed on the beach now, and the "bucanneers" were jumping off one by one.

First came Athanas, owner of the boat who we liked to call "Mr. Oui", oui being the only French word he knew. When he rented the boat to tourists, his abundant use of the word was accompanied by violent negative shakes of his head while he was bargaining on the price.

Billy jumped off next. He was the owner of a "chain" of discotheques as well as a pigsty containing forty sows.

Third came Apostolis, Billy's partner by night and barber by day.

The next one was helped off the boat. It was Constantis, the outdoor businessman." All his wares were hanging on his person: colourful worry beads, crosses, fisherman lighters and a large variety of other tourist goods. The back of his white jacket announced that he was the owner of "Tourist Enterprises - Mykonos - Greece."

His portable "shop", however, was not the reason he couldn't make it off the boat by himself. Constantis held a local record that nobody dared challenge: he was believed to have consumed, over the past forty years, more wine and ouzo than the entire population of the Cyclades islands.

Kyriakos, the best ex-tailor on the island, appeared next. He had retired three years ago and liked to explain that anyone who had worked with a needel and thread needed another lifetime to recover.

The last one off was Fouskis, a phenomenon among the local seamen. They say that the Myconites are expert seamen but can rarely swim. Fouskis did the swimming for all of them. After a hearty meal and several kilos of retsina, he returned home swimming, explaining that he was too drunk to walk home.

They were all between thirty and forty, except for Constantis who had stopped counting years ago.

Marilena watched them approaching the taverna like conquerors, which in a way they were. The land was theirs - they had conquered it with their strong and able hands. The sea was theirs they had conquered it since they were children and it had become their loving mother. As children, the sea had been their playmate; the sea had provided their food; the sound of the sea beating against the rocks had been their lullaby. Now, the sea provided the meze for their wine.

They had reached the taverna by now. Billy had an enormous octopus wound around his right arm. It was still alive, beating its tentacles wildly as Billy was trying to strangle it with two fingers.

"That's sadistic!" Marilena said. "Why doesn't he kill the poor thing and get it over with!"

Billy started to laugh, but he was touched by the look of pity on her face. With difficulty he unwound the octopus from around his arm, grabbed it by the tentacles and bit its neck savagely. He spit out the part left in his mouth and looked at Marilena as if he expected congratulations for his good deed.

"Now that the octapus has quieted down, why don't you relax too, sweetheart, and drink your wine?"

She took a sip, confused between feelings of relief and disgust. She tried to smile.

Calliope took the octapus and started beating it against the ground before grilling it.

Athanas emptied a bag full of sea-urchins and pinnas on the table. He started cracking the shells quickly and skillfully. The pinnas, split in two, with their entrails in half the shell, were drenched in oil.

"Oh, what's that little shrimp?" Marilena asked curiously.

"Pinnas, sweetheart, are these big big live shells, as you can see," Apostolis started to explain. "They're stuck at the bottom of the sea. When they're hungry, their shells open up like mouths. But it's dangerous, because pinnas can't see and, while their shells are open, a crab could get inside and eat them up. That's what the little shrimp is for - when it sees danger approaching, it bites the pinna's belly in warning and it closes up."

Marilena was astounded at nature's foresight. "If only people had a little shrimp to protect them ....." she mumbled.

"We'd probably eat it up, such beasts that we are" Athanas replied philosophically and went on splitting the shells.

By now the table looked like a fisherman's counter: sea-urchins, crab's feet, and pinnas were joined by the charcoal-grilled octapus that Calliope brought to the table.

Constantis, the alcoholic philosopher, as I liked to call him, was at his drunken best today. He had already started telling stories about his life to Marilena, who was an attentive listener.

He had lived his life on two islands. He was born on Mykonos and lived there when he wasn't at nearby Yaros, where he ended up every time he started a "business". Each time he was sent to the prison camp, he stayed for two or three years, depending on the offense. His "businessess" always had a disastrous end, but were amusing while they lasted.

One of his most imaginative enterprises had been the travelling theater group, which performed around the Cyclades islands in winter. All was going well, until one fateful Saturday night on Tinos. The theater was packed with islanders who had paid to see the performance. But they saw no performance. The company had dissolved, but Constantis couldn't bear to cancel a Saturday night performance, so he collected the money and tried to skip out. What he hadn't counted on, however, was that Tinos is an island with boat connections twice a week in winter. So it was easy for the local police to catch Constantis with the money in his pocket and to transfer him to the neighboring island of Yaros, free of change.

Constantis stated with pride that he had been "invited to the opening" of the island prison. He loved to tell these stories, and he had found the perfect audience in Marilena, who was listening in surprise and admiration for the courage with which he faced life.

Her greatest surprise, however, was when she heard that Constantis had memorized all of Seferis' works while "vacationing" on Yaros. The one that suited me most, during the endless, lonely days in prison, was the one that goes:

Meanwhile, empty and full wine bottles kept changing places at our table. The soft sea breeze, the endless, peaceful beauty all around us, together with the sweet dizziness in our heads, led us to contemplate dreamily that nothing could be better than the moments we were living now.

"Good company is like tomato sauce" Apostolis mused, "Both need wine to thicken smoothly ..."

Noone likes to be awakened in the middle of a pleasant dream, but Marilena was apparently on a different wave length. Now that I was in this condition, feeling that all the beauty in the world was near me, now that I could give up everything just to live on this island, no ...

"Let's go for a walk by the sea" Marilena's voice awakened me. "I want to talk to you."

It was like waking up with ice water being thrown in your face. The others looked at me and I could tell from their eyes that they understood.

"You're not going to last long with him, sweetheart' Athanas remarked and cursed at the sea-urchin that had pricked his finger. "Now that he's "anchored", nothing will get him up."

I had been afraid of this all along. Even if she wasn't in love with me, she had a fault common in all women: she could never be "with it" in a group like this. How did her mind work? Did she think she could get me up from where life was being so good to me, the cool breeze that chillec my wine, the people I liked around me, the feeling that an ocean separated me from the noises and the pollution of the city, from where only the sunlight told time, from where the sun embraces the sea ... Did she think she could get me up? To say what? To say: "You don't love me. You're not paying any attention to me ...."

No, it couldn't be true. There couldn't be people near me who lived in another world.

Nicolas, the driver, got up to go back to work, Marilena's words had been a forced landing into reality. But she still didn't understand.

"Why do you drink so much, Strati?" she inquired.

I gave her a straight answer, one that would shut her up: "Because when I drink I talk to the sea, and the sea tells me things that you couldn't."

Night had started falling. The sun was disappearing behind the cape. Everything was taking on a violet hue and the sun, calm now that it was falling, looked like an enormous lake spreading out to the golden-red mountains of Paros and Naxos.

"Time to start going back" someone said and we all got up eagerly. We were sleepy from the wine and the sun.

As soon as we were out of the bay, Athanas turned off the engine and silence spread all around. He raised the sails and the soft breeze was taking us slowly to the town's harbor.

I must have slept an hour, because when I woke up we were approaching the harbor and Athanas turned on the engines again.

"Are there many such days in a person's life?" Marilena asked, calmed by the peaceful joy of the trip back.

"Many" I answered, but only in Mykonos and only for those who have truly grasped the meaning of life - for those who have unwound the rope of happiness and made it a simple little piece of string. Happiness is simple and uncomplicated. It doesn't need many ingredients.

"Every day sparkling, luxurious yachts reach the island and we often think: How happy people must be in there. But it's not like that. Only the sailors are truly happy in there. But the people? I'm afraid that they need too much to be happy.

"What do you mean?" Marilena asked.

"I mean that in those beautiful yachts are things known as radiotelephones, and they spend most of the day holding the receiver in one hand and a Bloody Mary in the other. Their right hand gives them the bad news from their office of factory, or from the stock market. Then they take a few sips from the left hand to soothe the problems created by the right one."

Marilena laughed and I went on, "As soon as the gentlemen are temporarily finished with their business calls, their wives start communicating with the problems at home. The children, the governess, the servants, the gardener, the chauffeur, and whatever else the adversity of wealth carries along. Then the guests turn comes, and often the radiotelephones break down from all the use. Repair isn't easy, so in case of such bad luck they turn back immediately so they can confront their problems in person.

"I'd rather lose my right hand, than be emburdened with the happiness of yachts and chauffeurs and gardeners and stocks. You know what Constantis says when he sees a yacht. "There goes misery dressed in white ..."

CHAPTER 9

The days with Marilena rolled by in simple happiness. We went fishing, we drank with the boys, we played the philosopher. What Marilena enjoyed most were the endless discussions with Constantis over the poems of Seferis which resulted in giving the old man a new insight into the poets works and Marilena a detailed knowledge of living conditions on the island prison.

Emotionally, Marilena and I hadn't made an inch of progress. That is, I hadn't - she seemed to be falling more dangerously in love with me with every day that passed.

She was becoming almost neurotic, a condition that was aggrevated by the fact that I didn't go to bed with her. Although I had learned to enjoy her company in everything else, sexually she just didn't turn me on.

Returning home each night was beginning to be a problem. I felt obliged to make love to her, but I couldn't bring myself to do it. Often I would find common place excuses: When she was sleepy, I would tell her to go on to bed before me; when she was in a cheerful, drinking mood I would act sleepy and turn in for the night.

There was one other thing that bothered me about her. I knew close to nothing about her past. All I knew about her childhood was that she came from a wealthy middle-class family without many problems.

Fresh out of school, she had written a book, the one

she had sent me. I wished now that I had brought it along. It may have helped me understand her better if I could re-read the descriptions of her heroine. Trying to bring to mind some of the passages, I detected hints of an unstable personality that was surely based on her own.

Marilena was an unusual girl. I realized that, without meaning to, I was creating part of her problems. Perhaps I had led her to believe that some day she could be part of my life. Perhaps my carefree, "tomorrow is another day" manner was giving her hopes of more tomorrows ...

We had been in Mykonos for three carefree weeks, just sinking in the sun and the sea.

We had gone out fishing early that morning and returned home around five. Worn out from the sea and the wine, I dropped into bed and didn't get up until close to midnight. Marilena was out. Still drowsy, I got dressed and set out for Fouski's tavern.

Yes, it was definitely past midnight, I realized, because on the way I ran into Mr. Stink cleaning out the sewers. In Mykonos, the sewers get cleaned after midnight, and always by the same man, who has come to be known as Mr. Stink over the years.

The restaurant was empty, except for a couple of drunks who were under the impression that they were still having dinner. I sat down and ordered gigantes and a carafe of retsina. Soon another half kilo was sent my way from the other table. The wine was flowing from one table to the next when the inimitable mimis strolled in for his usual inspection of i.d. cards. This nightly round was his sleeping pill: if he didn't check out every single "suspect" on the island, he could sit up worrying all night. I was glad to have the crazy policeman join me - after drinking all day the retsina was hard on my stomach and I needed a partner.

"Your girl came by", the waiter told me "and had dinner with another girl." I was relieved that Marilena was well and had found company.

I paid and started towards billy's bar, bringing back memories with each whitewashed house that I passed ...It's strange, but Mykonos seems whiter in the dark than in sunlight. Even before electricity came to the island, night became day with the reflections from the whitewashed houses. On moonlit nights, the world's best "light man" couldn't duplicate the moon's effects on Mykonos.

Often I've been asked if I ever fell in love. "Head over heels", is always the answer, "with Mykonos."

Smiling to myself with the memory, I walked into Billy's bar. The lights were low, and so it was only after I had picked up my scotch from the bar that billy came to tell me that Marilena was sittin down with another girl. I turned my head and saw her relaxed on a sofa, chatting softly with another girl. I approached them and sat down.

"Have you met Alexandra, Strati?"

"No," I answered. "How are you, Alexandra?"

She murmured "fine" and turned back to Marilena. Her "fine" had been a strange one, as was the whole girl.

She wasn't more than 25. She was beautiful, with long black hair that met black eyes.

She was sitting down, and so I couldn't take a good look at her figure. But she seemed tall and well-proportioned.

Billy had the annoying habit of turning on the music very loud - to attract people, he explained - and so I couldn't hear what the two girls were talking about. I sat sipping on my scotch and watching two islanders dancing

44

a hasapiko. Every now and then I would turn to glance at the girls, but they seemed engrossed in their conversation.

I was a bit put off, but, then again, why should I care? Wasn't I the one who was getting tired of Marilena. So why should I care now that she wasn't talking to me? And yet, from time to time, I couldn't help glancing their way.

I'm an incurable egotist, it thought to myself. It's my hurt pride reacting this way.

Was I jealous of Marilena talking to someone else? Or was I attracted to Alexandra and jealous that Marilena was getting all her attention?

A little of both, I thought, along with a good measure of ego. I finished my scotch, told them I was going to piero's bar and left.

The music from Piero's bar was getting closer, but I had stopped on a corner, remembering old tarro who had died years ago. It was right on this corner, that she would leave her pot outside the door before turning in. In the middle of the night, she would get up, bring in the pot, pee and leave it by the door again. There were no sewers yet, so Mr. Stink would go around and emtpy the pots into his barrel.

Years ago, still in our teens, a group of us were fooling around in the night when we came across old tarro's pot. As if lightning had struck us, the same idea entered our heads: a practical joke - certainly not the first - on taro.

Within a few minutes, we had collected all the baking soda from our houses and emptied a few handfuls into the pot. We then hid in nearby corners, waiting for tarro's pee-time.

We didn't wait long. She got up, brought in the pot and then, beyond our most mischievous expectations, something truly fantastic happened.

When taro started peeing, the soda bubbled and - bubbled until it almost filled up her little room. Half asleep, the poor old woman was scared out of her wits by the phenomenon and stormed out into the streets yelling:

"Lord, I'm burning! Run people, run! My "thing" is on fire. It's foaming! Run, people, run!"

In an instant half the island was up. Shutters were opened; the neighbouring woman ran out with torches and candles. They could see the foaming pot and start yelling out curses and prayers: "Virgin mary, you burned her "thing", the cursed atheist!" Everyone ran back and forth, some were in hysterics, others ran to find a priest to exorcise her. In the midst of this madness, someone came up with a bright idea: take taro to the hospital on the nearby island of Syros.

By then we were out of our hiding places and of course we obliged. With everyone's blessings, we took old taro down to the harbor and, sure enough, found a caique ready to sail in spite of the late hour. Meanwhile, poor taro was running to and fro, her pants down, making air with her nightshirt to cool down. But just as we were about to sail off, enormous waves started breaking and it was impossible to move. And so we talked old taro into realizing that it was better to be alive with a scorched "thing" than drown in the angry sea. We turned back to the house.

As I strolled along my mind kept turning back to that strange girl with the wet eyes, to Marilena who for the first time hadn't winded herself up around me and to my annoying curiousity to hear what they were saying.

I reached piero's, which as usual was packed. I sat down on the edge of a (sofa) and didn't notice that there was a large group of foreigners next to me, drinking

46

champagne. Only when a champagne glass in a woman's hand came into my field of vision did I turn my head.

"Dark thoughts are bad for you", a girl said in English, extending the glass to me.

"Only her hair was dark" I answered and thought of Alexandra.

I took the glass, she took another one from the table and we clinked.

We exchanged toasts and emptied the glasses.

"See, I don't have dark hair to remind you of things", she said. "Better that way."

She refilled her glass. She got up, walked over to the bar and brought back another bottle of champagne, filling the glass again just as I had emptied it a second time.

A typically beautiful American. She had a Vigor about her that showed itself from the way she first talked to me. I liked her. The continuous depression with Marilena had made me feel like I was in mourning.

The "bang" of the next bottle brought me back to the present.

"What do they call you in America?" I asked her.

"The same as everywhere else: Jill."

"Is this your first time in Mykonos?"

The funny thing is that she asked me that question.

Probably the first time for you I answered, "or else you would have known me."

"And what's so important about you that I should know?"

"The ghost of manto (heirone of Greek revolution).

In within a half hour I had explained to her the highlights of the greek revolution. But unfortunately champagne makes me sleepy. I got up to say goodnight.

She was dizzy and didn't know what she was talking

about. And if there's one thing I can't stand, it's a drunk woman. She asked me if I'd like to join her on her boat for a swim the next day, but I told her that she and her friends could find me at the nudist beach every day and, no thanks, I would take my own boat - meaning, of course, Athanas' caique.

I walked home along the beach. I didn't think of stopping in at billy's to see if Marilena was still there. Actually, it crossed my mind, but I wanted to walk alone. I justified myself, thinking that by now she would surely be in bed. What's more, it was a chance to avoid the bothersome hints of when and whether we would sleep together.

The beach was empty and the sea was calm. The fishing boats stood absolutely still, as if they were parked cars. The sky was filled with stars; the moon, in its last quarter, was reddish and tilted.

"It'll be windy tomorrow", I thought to myself, turning into the little street that leads to the house.

I was walking absent-mindedly when I almost bumped into two shadows standing close together by the door. They didn't seem to have heard my footsteps.

I wasn't more than thirty steps away from them when the shock came. Instinctively, I stopped and withdrew slowly towards the wall. It was the two of them, but how! What I saw was hard to believe, and yet it was true. I was terrified, my hands were clammy and shaking.

Alexandra was kissing Marilena passionately, holding her tightly in her arms, her beautiful dark head leaning on Marilena's shoulder.

I had witnessed several such scenes, but only for kicks. Never with girls I cared about. Now my knees were trembling; it was hard to move but I had to.

This is my friend fouski .... in the sea sport outfit.

You must be very free in life to dance and sing when everything around you cries tied to the bond of an obligation. The only word Constadi had with God was when he asked to die standing". And that's how it happened, no illnesses, no beds.

"Great raffle ticket offer. A lamb and two lobsters ....." Poor Constadi.

A smile of love and two hands tightly held of friendship reflect the feelings of my nice friends on the island. This is "Nicholas" without his taxi.

Athanas the wolf. One of my nice good friends. He drives his rowboat with one hand, has one tooth, and knows the french "Oui" I mean he's unique.

The unforgetable Theodore father and protector of Peter of Pelekanou.
This photo was taken two hours before he died on Great Saturday in
1975.

It seems that Fouski's saying, leave us alone man. ......

Costa and his taxi. During the war we served in the same unit in the middle East.

The only thing I wanted was to leave without being seen, as if I were the guilty one. I crept silently into the dark, feeling like a thief who had almost been caught in the act.

CHAPTER 10

I couldn't pull myself together. The scene I had unexpectedly witnessed had left a deep impression on me. I walked briskly toward the sea, feeling as if I had run for miles.

Most of the cafes along the harbor were closed, but their tables and chairs remained on the sidewalk. I sat down at one of them, trying to recover. I just coudln't get over it.

Why be so upset, I asked myself. After all, Marilena didn't interest me that way - I had hardly ever kissed her. Her sex life was not my concern ... But that wasn't my problem, I realized. It wasn't either Marilena or my hurt egotism that caused this turmoil inside me.

It was Alexandra. I coudln't allow myself to face it, but it became clearer and clearer. I had left Billy's bar because Alexandra had ignored me. I had left the pretty American girl at Piero's, because Alexandra was on my mind. What was the matter with me? Was it love at first sight? But it couldn't be! I had merely sat near her for a few minutes, and she hardly looked my way. Not even adolescents fall in love like that any more!

So what was the matter? I couldn't find a feasible explanation. Alright, so her wet black eyes were like magnets. So what? I tried to be honest with myself - could it be my hurt pride again? Yes, that was it. I wanted her, but she wanted Marilena and not me. I didn't want Marilena, but she was mine - she was my intellectual possession. Now Alexandra had her, too. Had those eyes conquered us both?

The scene I had inadvertently witnessed had aroused my mind, my body, my very being. I had to admit it. I wanted Alexandra passionately. But how was I to have her?

She belonged in another world, she was a different form of sexual being. For me, it was the worst form of unsatisfied love and a tortured ego. It was despair without any hope. Since I wanted her so badly, I would have to survive an illegitimate experience.

Yes, the decision was made. I would play a humiliating role simply so I could be near her. I would return home, and not only keep Marilena there, but invite Alexandra as well. I was creating a novel of love and adventure and the idea had a tragic charm about it.

My mind was made up. I've always believed that a man is responsible for his acts - not guilty of them - and responsible people are aware of the consequences. Isn't morality, after all, based on the idea that the consequences of an act make it legal?

So I decided to return home. If Alexandra came, I was ready to bear the consequences. I started walking back slowly, a smile of contentment on my face.

I had won over my initial reactions. The smile was one of sarcasm, directed at myself. My despair had found its hope. I didn't believe in morality; I considered it an outdated, stiff form of religion.

What I was interested in was to experience the power that creates new spheres of fantasy; to be liberated from the erotic ghosts that haunted me since I met Alexandra;

to live in the presence of carnal truth. Voluntarily I would create and respect a paranoiac condition in my house, which would force me to maintain a disinterested stand if I wanted to safeguard my manhood. You could call it self-respect. You could even call it masochism.

But it was neither one nor the other. It was a period of trial for love and passion, the very essence of the splendor and futility of human life.

CHAPTER 11

Everything had happened suddenly that night. After analyzing the situation and drawing conclusions, I expected to spend a peaceful night, in anticipation of the next day when I would put my plan into action. Little did I expect what was to follow.

When I got home Marilena was in her bed smoking.

"Haven't you gone to sleep yet?" I asked her.

"I've had nightmares she answered stupidly".

Neither of us spoke after that. I got into bed and started reading the "Advice to the Lovelorn" colomn of a popular magazine. I was in the middle of "Eve's" answer to the girl whose fiancee was going out with her best friend, when I looked up.

Marilena was standing by my bed, nude.

I looked back at the magazine.

"I want to make love with you" she announced in a tone that indicated she had tortured herself before reaching the point of telling me.

Without looking at her, I answered calmly:

'   "Marilena, please go back to your bed and try to attain what you want in life, for whatever reason you want it, without humiliating yourself."

"What do you mean, for whatever reason I want it?" she asked, obviously bothered. She put something on.

I felt badly when I saw her blushing. She seemed at a

loss to explain her own actions.

"There's a motive in everything we do", I went on. "That's what I mean by "for whatever reason you want it". When we try to achieve something, we always have a reason, be it love, emotion, or that we want to suppress another emotion which is about to engulf us."

She opened her eyes wide - what I meant was obvious. But how could I be referring to something that she alone knew? In the ten minutes I had spent with them, I couldn't have noticed anything. Her mind worked quickly. She concluded that I couldn't possible know anything.

"You must be extremely stupid if you haven't realized how I feel about you" she said in an annoyed tone.

After losing her dignity, she was losing her self-control, too. The conversation was becoming very unpleasant.

"If we can't keep this civilized, I'd rather go to sleep" I said and went to turn off the light.

That was all she needed! Another Marilena, one I had never seen before, revealed herself. She had been hurt and humiliated. She had offered to make love because she felt she was going astray, and I had refused her. Emotionally, she had lost control, not knowing where the adventure she was starting out on with Alexandra would lead, and she was trying to find something that might save her. Her face had become red with anger; she had become a different person.

"What kind of a person are you, anyway? she screamed in anger, "what kind of a beast are you? What do you think you'll gain by humiliating me? What are you trying to prove? That you're the strong one? That feminine wiles are indifferent to you? That you can have any woman you want, whenever you want her? That when you have her you couldn't care less? why did you bring me here? To meet your drunken friends? At least they respect their women! What are you, anyway? tell me! Tou're queer, that's it! You're a godamn homosexual! There's no other explanation! That's why you don't want me!

Her eyes were those of a mad woman. She didn't know what she was saying. Or maybe she did know - because this was no longer hysteria, it was a stupid form of blackmail! Me, homosexual? Just because I didn't want to fuck her?

As I was sitting up and she was yelling in my ear, my hand, almost of its own will, whipped with force against her face. She landed in a corner, her screams mixed with tears:

"I feel sorry for you! I really pity you!" she wailed.

I turned off the light, thinking that she ought to reserve her pity for herself - she needed it more. The episode had temporarily taken Alexandra off my mind, so I fell quickly into a deep sleep.

The next morning, she came cheerfully into my room with breakfast and kissed me on the cheek. she had the look of someone who had reached a decision after much thought. Her words confirmed it:

"Do you mind if we take Alexandra along to the beach?"

"Of course not! Great idea!"

It was obvious that we both wanted Alexandra, each one for a different reason. We would make a splendid trio!

Out of plain curiosity, I asked her how she had met Alexandra.

"She was alone at Billy's and we started talking."

"And what is this Alexandra?" I persisted.

"What do you mean, what is she? She's a girl studying law and she's here on vacation."

"I'm asking because I never saw her in Mykonos before."

"Sorry, she forgot to ask you for a visa."

"Listen, Marilena, I can't stand this kind of conversation so early in the morning. Go pick up your friend and bring her here so we can start off."

I took a sip of coffee and lit another cigarette.

Alexandra was staying at one of the houses that rent rooms. Marilena soon returned with her. In the daylight she looked even more beautiful.

She went around the house and let out a gasp of admiration every once in a while. Not that the house was that special, but she had apparently never been in a real home in Mykonos before and expected them all to be like the one that rented rooms.... when she went out on the terrace, which is built on the sea, she shouted in delight:

"Oh! But this isn't Mykonos! It's Venice!"

"This part of town is called Venice, didn't you know?" I explained.

I had brought Alexandra to the house in accordance with my plan. Without looking at Marilena, while we were watching the fish gathering in search of food, I asked her:

"Do you fish?"

"No, but I'd like to learn."

"Good! Then you can come and stay here and get up early in the morning so you can catch fish and fry them for breakfast!"

Immediately they threw a quick glance at one another - Alexandra with a look of unexpected joy, Marilena with surprise. She knew that it wasn't easy for me to live with a woman, let alone two of them.

"Are you serious?" she asked me.

"Why not! As long as she's tidy and doesn't let the

bathtub overflow."

Alexandra threw a guilty glance my way. We were all hiding something from one another.

We set off for the beach and decided to pick up Alexandra's things on the way back. Along the way, Stavros, the taxi driver, picked us up.

I saw you walking like Christ between two bandits, he said, so I thought you could use a dip in the sea to cool off!"

"I think "like a bandit between two Christs" is more suitable", Marilena laughingly corrected him.

I got in the front of the cab, next to Stavros, and left the two of them in back. We headed towards Calamopodi where, according to Stavros' exclusive information, we could find freshly caught fish.

Calamopodi is an endless golden beach that foreign visitors have justly re-named "Paradise". Thankfully, no first-class restaurants, luxurious villas or other monstrosities that destroy the island's natural beauty have cropped up here yet.

As I was thinking about what "progress" is doing to Mykonos and the islands in general, we had reached the summit from where we could see the coastline and we were descending towards the sea. Thoughts about the landscape were in my mind but my ears were focused on the back seat. I wanted to know what was happening, and why.

Marilena was clearly heterosexual. Could an unsatisfied love, which she perhaps felt for me, have transformed her into a lesbian? Or perhaps was this leap to the other side of the sexual game a well-acted ploy? Was she playing her last card, trying to stimulate my feelings of jealousy or pride?

Marilena had lost the game, of course, and she was living in the panic of the opponent who's way behind. As for myself, I felt that I had won a one-sided duel. I could enter the next round.

Marilena, not willing to face her defeat, was still throwing her poisoned arrows. We had reached Paradise, the island's most famous nudist beach.

"Do you still swim nude at your age? she asked sarcastically, trying to punish me for my first step towards victory. She wanted to laugh at my age, unable to see anything else to laugh at. I was fiftyish, but didn't look it.

My conscience had prepared me for the attack - anyone conscious of reality cannot be surprised by the mention of his age. But Marilena felt I had to be punished and I accepted the rules of her game, so I undressed and went towards the sea. The cold salt water cooled me off and affected me in mind and body. Everything looked beautiful - especially Alexandra, who was standing nude and talking to Marilena.

She was truly gorgeous. It wasn't just my imagination - all it had done was make me want her so much. I felt primitive, wishing I could swoop her in my arms and take her into the cool water with me. I wanted to make love to her savagely, but I knew this wasn't the time and place.

I swam back to the beach and lay down, letting the sun dry me. All along the beach, people of all ages, all sizes and shapes, all races, were enjoying the sun's embraces. For the newcomer under, say, sixty, the scene may have been a turn-on. But like everything else, you get used to nudity - even some of the sexually undernourished Greeks do the whole scene and it has a purity about it, and within a quarter of an hour even the oglers have stripped, their last trace of curiosity or embarrassment gone.

During the summer, Paradise beach is inhabited by several hundred young people, mostly foreigners, who live close to nature. They set up their tents, one shop for cold cuts and beer from Freddy's little grocery. The only thing that might upset their peaceful, simple life on the beach is the Law, with a capital L.

The Law! I felt sorry for the law enforcement officers on the island who have to do their duty: and wipe out sin, even if it doesn't really exist. In order to wipe out sinners - in this case the nudists - he has to arrest them in the nude. That can be very difficult, however, because it's easy to spot someone in uniform on a nudist beach, and just throw a towel over the "forbidden" parts.

So the Law has to camouflage itself, by looking like everyone else on the beach: nude. Being a prude, the Law cannot totally strip down. So it does the next best thing: the officers wear a swimsuit, usually black, its shape depending on the shape of the previous user. The suit belongs to the police department and is thus worn by whichever officer is on duty at Paradise beach.

The officers always keep their socks and shoes on, too, both black to match the suit. Obviously, they may as well have kept their uniforms on - black socks and shoes are not the most discreet cover-up on a nudist beach. So, the Law is almost always unsuccessful, unless some innocent nudist has fallen asleep without noticing its presence. Triumphant, the Law stands over his or her head, utters a discreet "Hey you, prison!", menacingly dangling a pair of handcuffs. It takes some time before the once happy tourist realizes it is not just a bad dream ...

By that time, the handcuffs are already on him and the Law is ordering him to get dressed. But how? Now, the officer has a problem. If he takes off the handcuffs, he's afraid the sinner might run into the sea, in which case he will have to enlist the aid of the harbor master, the only representative of the Law who might know how to swim. So the officer, not wanting someone else to reap the rewards of the arrest, comes up with a solution. He takes off one handcuff and puts it around his own wrist, thus leaving the criminal with one free hand with which to dress. Momentarily linked together, both attempt to clothe themselves with one hand. They link ends as soon as they are dressed. They leave together, the one triumphant, the other still not knowing what hit him ...

CHAPTER 12

Alexandra and Marilena came out of the sea together and lay down next to me. Alexandra had the most perfect body I'd ever seen, more beautiful even than the lithe Scandinavian girls on the beach.

The three of us were lying silently close to one another, enjoying the hot sun on our wet bodies. Each of us was probably thinking of what the outcome of our trio might be.

We might be considered an abnormal trio, if one considers lesbianism a perversion. Being as normal as can be, how had I come to fall in love with a lesbian, I asked myself. The more I saw of her, the more I wanted her. Certainly my desire wasn't a perverted one - Alexandra was a woman, and a very beautiful woman at that. So she liked woman - what did I care? It was her problem.

My own problem was much simpler: she didn't want me and would probably never want me. Never! It seemed too long a time to wait, but like any good hunter, I knew that waiting was part of the game. I wanted Alexandra, and I would wait for her.

The sun got tired of shining down on us and hid behind the clouds. We got up and went towards the restaurant. Fresh fish, the salty sea breeze, and Alexandra it was all a man could want.

Now she was looking at me too. Was it guilt I detected

in her smoldering eyes? No, it couldn't be. She looked only at women with guilt.

While the two of them were eating and chatting and laughing gaily, I was drinking more and more, trying to fill up the void in my stomach, that special void that comes only when you're in love. My mind was lost in a dark labyrinth and only their laughter brought me occasionally back to reality.

The sun was shining once more and we ran into the sea. They wanted to cool off; I wanted to clear my confused head. It felt so good to be under water; I felt like staying there forever. When I finally decided to surface, Alexandra was standing over me. Hardly able to see from the water in my eyes, I reached out for her and she wound up in my arms.

The feel of her wet body on mine was more exciting than anything I'd ever felt. I held her tightly and looked into her eyes. I couldn't explain the look in them. Was it guilt? Or was it suprise? Yes, it was a guilty, surprised look. She had her arms around me, too. Stupidly, I thought it meant something, even though it was a natural thing to do - did I expect her to let her arms just hang? Surely I was going out of my mind ......

I was still holding Alexandra when she did something unbelievable: She raised her arms from around my back and wound them around my neck, pressing her wet face close to mine.

I was paralyzed. My bones seemed to have moved away from the sockets. I tried to make the moment last as long as possible. With our arms still around each other, we tumbled into the sea, laughing. We got out again. She took a deep breath and swam away. I walked back to the beach, where Marilena was laughing with our games.

Games? Was that all it meant? She swam towards Alexandra while I stood there, motionless. I don't know how long I stayed that way, totally mixed up.

Margo, an Australian girl who comes to Mykonos every summer, came near me.

"Hey, what's the matter?" she asked.

"Nothing ... nothing." I didn't know what else to answer. I hardly knew what was wrong with me. Margo and I walked along the beach, but my mind and eyes were on the two girls swimming. Alexandra came out first.

"She must be jealous", I thought and laughed at myself for having gotten so ridiculous.

Just as the girls came back, Nicola's caique was approaching and we decided to leave. The sun was down, and we were all tired. The boat set off. We sat quietly, watching the red sun sinking into the sea.

On the other side of the boat, a black American lay with a blonde on either side. He had an arm around each of them. I compared him with myself. I wasn't black, but we both had two girls. Or rather, he did. I had none. I wanted one of the two with me, but didn't know whother I could ever have her.

Tired from thinking the same things over and over again, tired from the sun and the wine, I went straight to bed when we got home. The fatigue was stronger than the anxiety. I dropped off to sleep.

CHAPTER 13

Alexandra lived at my place now.

When I woke up I saw a light in the next room. I could hear no sounds and I went to take a look. There was no one in the room. Alexandra's things were hanging from the tacks on the wall. Her bed wasn't made up; the shape of her body was still on it. I stroked the pillow and leaned down to get a whiff of the salty smell of her body.

Suddenly I heard the door open. For a second I was petrified, afraid of getting caught. I ran into the bathroom. Rarely in my life had I felt so embarrassed. But, I wondered, would it perhaps have been better if Alexandra had found me there, stroking the outline of her body on the sheets? She would have had to face my problem, and that would have meant a definite change in the situation ... for better or for worse.

Still in the bathroom, I could hear them talking outside. I decided to take a bath, and shampoo my hair. Feeling purified, I walked out with a towel around my waist. I went out to the terrace where the girls were having a drink.

"Hi, there!" I said happily, for I was really happy to have them with me. "Don't I deserve a drink?"

They both rushed to get another glass, ice and water. The scotch bottle was already on the table. The evening's first drink is a special one - it can make or break the rest

Apostoli, "Apostoli the butt" always good wines, good fish and a big kind heart.

Nice things. Fouski with Athana.

Jimmy O'conor, life and common ...... society, the most loyal Ireland man of Mykonos, he walks together with Michael the wolf.

"Apostolis' butt" during a midday relaxation.

The fishing boat brought in a lot of "stuff" that morning.

Kaliopis' little tavern in Psarou, behind the canes, closed though, September just came in.

Billy at a feast.

The "Public" popular orchestra of Mykonos with Peter the negro the conductor. The violin is Stradivarious.

of the night. So they fixed me a tall, stiff scotch with plenty of ice.

I sipped on my drink with delight, enjoying the cool evening breeze after a tiresome, hot day. I was relaxed. The sky was full of stars; from the ills across, the moon was rising behind a windmill. The sea beneath the terrace was playing with the rocks, which were the natural foundations of the house.

The feeling of joy had overcome my anxiety. I remembered that earlier today, the fatigue had overcome my the anxiety - thus only my emotional and sexual needs were heightened by Alexandra. But wasn't that enough. And isn't desire a kind of happiness in itself? It gave me a purpose. Every day, I woke up wondering if I'd be able to make the next step. Happiness is always relative, it never takes the same form.

Suddenly I saw fires lighting across the bay. I jumped up.

"Com'n, let's go" I said.

"What's wrong?" they asked me simultaneously, sounding worried.

"Let's go, let's go" I repeated and downed my scotch in one gulp.

"But what's the matter?" they repeated.

"Nothing's the matter. There's a festival tonight, at St. John's across. Let's go have some fun!"

The girls were delighted. They grabbed sweaters - there's no such thing as a warm night in Mykonos - and the three of us set out.

Marilena looked happier, at peace with herself now. Perhaps because I, too, felt better. I don't know what she assumed, but my better disposition affected her positively. I was absolutely sure by now that her relationship with

65

Alexandra was a reaction to my indifference toward her. Either way, I didn't care. Alexandra was all I longed for.

When we got to the square, I saw Nicolas taxi, locked up for the night. His house was close by and I saw the lights on. I knocked on the door.

"Hey, who's that?" he shouted and I could tell that his mouth was full.

"The slob's eating again I thought and pushed the door open. He was seated at a table in the middle of the room, eating from two plates. His wife was bringing out more food.

Sit down and eat he said between mouthfuls.

"Stop eating and get up so we can go to the feast, I barked at him. Nicolas stopped chewing, his mouth open with the last mouthful clearly visible.

"I had forgotten all about it! he exclaimed. "How could I forget St. John's?" he kept on asking himself.

He took a napkin and wiped the sauce from his mouth. Just as he was pushing back his chair to get up, his wife Annouso came from the kitchen, carrying a bowl of skordalia. The smell of garlic filled the room.

"Where do you think you're going, you loafer?" she snapped at him.

"Shut up! I've got work".

"What do you mean work, at this time of night?"

"I'm taking the man to St. John's, so keep quiet!"

Annouso cursed St. John up in heaven and then asked for forgiveness, crossing herself, while Nicolas laughed and took a last bite.

"Goodnight, Annouso" I said going out the door.

"Go to the devil!" she yelled. "You won't even let the poor man eat his dinner in peace!"

Nicolas and I walked out in fits of laughter.

Marilena and Alexandra were walking up and down the little square, their arms around each other, talking and laughing. I wondered what might have happened in the afternoon, while I was in deep sleep. They looked happy together .... they looked almost in love.

Nicolas unlocked the car and I sat in my usual seat, next to him. We started up the road towards the village. Groups of people were going to the feast on foot. Around the cape's bend, bonfires and candles from St. John's monastery were seen. St. John's was like all the island's little chapels: a big verandah facing the sea in front. Long tables all around where the villagers were sitting and drinking from the demijohns piled together in the cell. The women were huddled over the big kettle, watching the lamb cook. Religious feasts are the only occasion on which lamb is eaten boiled, and for a very good reason: the soup after a long night of drinking is like milk for the ulcer.

The road ended some 200 meters before the church. As we came out of the car, the soft wind slapping our faces totally revived us. The drunken voices of friends and strangers came closer and closer.

"They're going to get the saint drunk again tonight" Nicolas said, adding that we could do as we pleased - St. John shouldn't have become a saint if he wanted the right to get drunk.

"Com'n, Nicolas", I answered for the saint. "It's his nameday tonight. Let him drink to his heart's content for once!"

Our friends saw us immediately. Whoever said that drunks can't see? They made room for us to sit and put glasses filled to the rim in front of us.

The musicians were playing island songs, while the

young girls were dancing. It was still early for the men to get up. They were still drinking to the Saint's health. The priest, too, was drinking now, to cool his throat from the psalms to the saint.

"Go see if the lamb is ready", he said to his wife, and as soon as she was gone he reached out to fondle the chanter's niece. The girl blushed and kissed his holy hand, when his wife re-appeared, carrying half the lamb in the pan. She placed it in front of him.

The holy hands, in the young girl's breast a minute ago, were now tearing the lamb's leg in two. Soon, a dozen hands were grabbing at the lamb, tearing at its crunchy skin and bones. After each bite, they would pick up their wine glasses to wash down the fatty meat.

Alexandra and Marilena were watching in a disgusted sort of winder. Personally, I was fascinated by this primitive Greek Vigor.

When their hunger was satisfied, they got up to start the dancing:

I'm gonna buy you a boat
So you can sail about,
So everyone can shout:
There goes the captain's woman,
I'm gonna buy you a boat
So the stars can say good night
So you can be greeted by the stars at night
and by the sea-birds when it's light.

The voices and the instruments tore through the night, reaching up to St. John in his heavenly abode.

When daylight came, the soup kettle was brought out to calm down the stomachs acid from all the wine. The sun was rising, and the early morning's peace matched the peace in our minds and stomachs. Some started slowly home, softly singing, while others rested their heads against the softness of their women. God bless St. John!

CHAPTER 14

We slept late the next morning, and woke up each in his own bed. Sex was at a deadlock in this house!

"It's all I deserve, the way I managed to mix everything up", I thought, I was getting angry with myself which I had always praised for being cool and logica. How had I gotten involved like this? I had always known exactly what I wanted and where I was going. And now? I knew now, too, of course. I wanted Alexandra. And I was standing very firmly on the ground, wanting to know if she wanted Marilena.

If at any moment I didn't feel up to the struggle necessary to get what I wanted, I could always pack up and go back to Athens - but I realized that escape needed more courage than staying and waiting.

Meanwhile, life at home had drifted into a routine. Every morning, the girls would make my coffee, while I sat in the next room writing, playing the role of the all-knowing author and akwardly laugh at myself. Humor, after all, was my only consolation.

We had decided not to go to the beach that day. I spent the day reading and trying to write without being able to continue, not daring to think of what the end might be. I was frightened of the outcome.

I lay down, staring at the wooden beams of the ceiling. It must have been about five o'clock when I fell asleep. I woke up several hours later - or, rather, I was awakened by the sound of the waves beating against the house. The weather had suddenly changed that afternoon.

The girls were sitting on the terrace. huddled close together. They seemed to be protecting one another from the angry sea. An enormous wave broke on the terrace and its white froth drenched their faces.

Marilena let out a little cry and turned to look at me. She looked as if she may have been crying, with the water streaming down her face. Perhaps she really had cried. There was a turmoil in her mind and in her heart, and I was unable to help. I felt guilty, but only until Alexandra looked at me. She, too, was wet, but she was smiling. I threw them a towel and went into the house.

I sat at my desk and looked at the sea absent-mindedly. The sky was black; not a star could be seen. I sat there for a long time, staring with awe at the anger of nature. It wasn't the first time I was witnessing a storm in Mykonos, but now my state of mind was such that the raging sea terrified me. I found it a bad omen.

I realized after seeing them on the terrace together that way, that they would no longer try to hide their feelings from me. I was frightened at what would inevitably happen - perhaps even tonight. I felt a strong urge to look at how things were proceeding out there, but my egotism and my pseude-dignity stopped me.

I tried to read, to write, to think clearly. It was futile. All I managed to do was smoke all the cigarettes left in my pack and to stare at the sea's wrath.

The fact that I was out of cigarettes was a good excuse to leave the house. I walked along the harbor. The wind was raging and the street was empty and wet from the waves that had splashed it. I bought cigarettes and walked into the "Cabin", a bar housed in the building that was once the island's Venetian prison.

Bobby, the owner, looked at me in surprise. My face must have revealed how I felt. In order to avoid the question that was sure to come, I remarked;

"Big storm tonight".

"It looks that way", he answered. "Looks like you're seasick."

"Well, then, give me a double scotch. It might help me recover."

Bobby didn't say a word. He poured my drink.

"You know something?" he asked, coming near me.

"What?"

"You've got too many worries, and that's no good. No one's going to live long enough to solve the world's problems."

I was in no mood for conversation, simply because I couldn't talk to Bobby about my problems. Any islander would consider them shameful.

"Remember old Sarantos?" he went on.

"Sure I do."

"Well, he had a lot of problems. All kinds of problems. He never enjoyed anything in life, and he died worrying about other people's problems. He bought houses for all the members of his family, he bought them land, he married off his daughters and grandaughters, and on his deathbed, he still had problems. He asked for his children and grandhildren to gather round him.

"Bring me Evanthia and Erato, my daughters", he said. They came. "Bring me my grandchildren, too", he said. They came and he kissed each one of them. "Bring me my son, Nicolas", he said. He came. "Where's your son, Apostolis? the old man asked him. "He's here, too, father".

"Then who's minding the store?" old Sarantos shouted angrily. He died that way, furious because no one was minding the store."

I smiled, because my problems were totally different from those of old Sarantos. I asked for another drink.

Constantis, the fisherman, walked in just then.

"What a storm! The sea's going to drown us all!" he exclaimed and ordered a drink. As soon as he gulped it down, he turned to me: "Where are your women tonight, boss?"

I was annoyed by his choice of words.

"What do you mean, my women?"

"Well, you're always with one or the other of them, that's why I asked" he explained.

"The're home. This is no weather to be out."

"Then have another drink, and then let's go have some fish soup."

Constantis' company was just what I needed tonight. He left for Tzanni's taverna, near the jetty. Even before we opened the door, the smell of fish frying was in the air. We sat at a table near the window. Drops of sea water splashed the panes from time to time.

It was the first squall of the season.

"Heavy weather", Constantis said. "The sudden change, so quickly, always gets on my nerves."

He took a sip of wine and went on:

"I don't mind the storm, but the way it was beautiful this morning and now this, it's like a warning of what we'll go through for the next six or seven months. In the middle of winter, you count the days left until spring, then summer. It's the beginning of winter that's hard: everything looks dark and dreary."

I listened to Constantis quietly, then asked him if he'd

ever been to Paris.

"You mean to France."

"Yes, but to Paris"

"I've been to Marseilles. The ship never docked in Paris."

"How can the ship have docked, you fool! Paris isn't a port!"

"Well, then I haven't been there."

"Listen, there's a river that runs through Paris, the Seine. In the middle of the river, there's an islet which has big and beautiful houses, wealthy houses. The wealthiest Parisians live there, because the river is all around and the view is beautiful. It's called St. Ludwig's island."

"Of course! The wealthy always want a saint who can look after their money!"

"As I was saying, the houses are built on a kind of mole to protect their foundations. So on this mole, the "chochars" have set themselves up. They've been there for many years, because the rich used to throw their leftovers at them. That's the way they lived."

Constantis was listening carefully, taking an occasional sip of wine.

"The clochars, my friend, are a strange species. They're something like tramps, but they're not tramps. They're people who used to be important - professors, philosophers, rich people who lost everything, and so on. Now they live there in groups, like families."

"These things really happen in Paris! You must be kidding!"

"Not only do they happen, but they're considered a tourist attraction! Anyhow, once I was staying at a house on St. Ludwig's and I could watch them from above. It was fall, like now, and they feel the same way you do about the oncoming winter. Every year there are a few who decide they can't take it any longer."

"So what do they do", he asked, full of curiosity.

"When someone decides he's through, he tells the others. When night starts falling, a kind of celebration begins. After several hours of heavy drinking, he gets up and kisses his closest friends. Everyone watches silently. Not a sound can be heard, and in this absolute stillness, a loud splash is heard - it's the sound of the body falling into the freezing water. No one speaks, no one cries. They just go to sleep."

Constantis didn't say a word. He just looked at me, thinking who knows what. He didn't tell me what he was thinking. Instead, he ordered the soup. As we were eating, he repeated:

"It's a dangerous time of year."

He seemed to have been deeply influenced by the story I'd told him. He hardly opened his mouth the rest of the night. We finished our meal an went out. The weather was getting worse by the minute. The waves looked like enormous black figures in the night, menacingly approaching the harbor. At some point we parted and I headed towards the house. I was in agony; my knees were trembling. I tried to keep away my dark thoughts, telling myself that it was just my sexually disturbed imagination, that the girls would be in their separate beds, that sooner or later everything would work out with Alexandra. It was no use.

I approached the house warily, feeling like a thief about to break in. I turned the key softly and tiptoed into the house. There were no lights on. Waves were still breaking on the terrace, and their sound muffled my footsteps. I went towards my room and tried to see if Marilena was in her bed. Fumbling in the dark, I realized the bed was empty. I was dumb founded; I didn't dare turn on the light.

I tiptoed out of the room again and, like a sleepwalker, headed towards Alexandra's room. The door was closed. Unable to move, I stood there with my hand on the doorknob. I wanted to run, but my legs disobeyed. What I was afraid of, had happened .... was happening right now.

Just as I was about to attempt returning to my solitary bed, a sigh, and then another, permeated the sea's humming. Whispers were heard, but I couldn't make out the words.

I was afraid they had heard me, but realized it was impossible. They were too busy making love. The sounds of their embraces tore through the dreadful night like the stammerings of a dying man.

Why had I made myself go through this terrible experience? Why hadn't I found another girl tonight, a girl to sleep with somewhere else? I wanted to, but couldn't. I was in love with Alexandra, and I was suffering. Did I want to suffer? Was this my perversion? I smiled in my misery, at the irony of thinking of myself perverted, when right behind the door, the perversion of the girl I loved was reaching its climax. Now they could be heard clearly.

"You'll be with me always ..."

And Marilena's sad, passionate reply:

"Yes, now I love you. I came into your arms with bitterness, but now I love you ..."

My mouth was dry. My temples were about to burst. I don't know how long I stood there, transfixed. I wanted desperately to leave, but I had to hear it all ... the sighs, the cries of pleasure, the words of love.

Daylight started creeping through the window. I dragged myself to bed, knowing that sleep was impossible.

CHAPTER 15

I must have fallen asleep. I thought I heard the telephone ringing, not knowing whether I was awake or dreaming. I didn't get up. The ringing stopped after a while, or maybe someone had picked up the receiver. I went back to my troubled sleep.

It was almost noon when I woke up to face the dreadful day ahead. How would I face the situation? How would I comfront the girls, being hopelessly in love with one, feeling terribly guilty toward the other, hating them both for what was going on between them? Could I possibly act as if I knew nothing? I knew I wasn't that talented an actor. They would realize that I knew, they would make fun of me. I was ashamed of myself, of what I had gotten myself into.

My first glance went to Marilena's bed. Had she returned, or was she still in Alexandra's arms. The bed was empty, neatly made up from the day before. Were they both so shameless that they ignored my presence in this house?

I got up to go to the bathroom. Alexandra's door was half-open. They must have gone out earlier, I thought. Now I wouldn't even have company. Cautiously, I looked into the room, not wanting to face the scene of the crime.

Alexandra was sleeping, alone. She was nude and uncovered. The bed looked as if a horde of barbarians had passed through. The sheets were crumpled in a corner and, next to them, Alexandra was lying, worn out but still beautiful, her ebony hair covering half her face.

Marilena must have gone shopping, I thought. I stood there, looking at Alexandra in her sleep. I wanted her dreadfully, but I didn't dare. I was afraid of being turned down.

I left her lying there and went to make coffee. The table was set for two. I wondered why. Then I saw a note on the table. I picked it up.

"My darling", it started. It was Marilena's handwriting, and I assumed it was addressed to Alexandra. "I left early to catch the first plane.

My brother was injured in a car accident, but it's not serious. I'll call you from Athens. I hope you don't get bored alone in the house."

So it was probably for me. Anyhow, I was sorry about her brother, but since it wasn't serious I was glad to have her out of the way for a while. Perhaps without her, I could somehow make it with Alexandra.

It was a strange note. The "my darling" didn't mean much, of course. But what did she mean by I hope you don't get bored alone?" Did she really mean it, or was she joking? Had she realized that I was waiting for just such a chance. I remembered what she'd been saying to Alexandra the night before about "bitterness". Had she made love with Alexandra to make me jealous or to turn her emotions elsewhere? Judging from the note, she hadn't gotten very far. Suddenly I felt sorry for her, because she left knowing that I wanted Alexandra.

Meanwhile the water was boiling and I made two cups of coffee. Now I had a reason to wake Alexandra. I had news, important news for her. I took the coffee into her room, put them on the table and sat on her bed. I wanted to wake her up with a kiss, but she had already opened her eyes. She blinked a few times, as if she wondered what I was doing there.

"A strong cup of coffee is what you need", I said and handed her a cup. She took a sip and looked for her cigarettes. I gave her the one I had just lit. She inhaled and looked into my eyes. God! Those eyes! Even now, they were gorgeous! I had never seen a woman before who looked so beautiful when she woke up.

"Marilena left", I informed her in a voice that contained indifference, joy, a little sadness and a lot of hope.

"She abandoned us both?" Her tone was clearly sarcastic. She was a strong girl emotionally, and that's one of the things that made her so attractive.

"I would think she abandoned only you, because she didn't have anything going with me", I answered in a similar tone.

"It doesn't make any difference what you had going. What you have inside counts."

"I don't know how much you've understood, nor what you mean."

"I haven't understood all that much", she answered, "but you're the one who understands nothing."

It was an attack; there was no going back now. The chance I'd been looking for to clear matters up was here, right after a night of torture. How right the fishermen were: clear skies always follow the storm!

"Read this and tell me what you think", I said handing her the note.

She read it, always with the same sarcastic look on her face. "You see", she said, looking straight into my eyes,

"You're the one she calls "My darling". As to the "I hope you don't get bored", that shows that she's aware of your feeling guilty. Or did you think you're a genius surrounded by mentally retarded women?"

"Did you think", she went on revealingly, "that Marilena, who's come to know you well, or even I, knowing you for such a short time, ever thought you were taking us both in out of sheer kindness? You brought two women into your house, who in a way upset your habits, your noon siestas, your neatly organized life, just because you took a liking to your friend's friend? Com'n, Strati, don't underestimate your enemies so much!"

"So now we're enemies? I said, and immediately realized it was a stupid question. In any case, she was leading the conversation right where I wanted it.

"It's not "now" that we've become enemies. We were enemies right from the beginning."

The conversation was taking on a wily tone that I found intriguing. Things were turning out the way I wanted them, or so I thought. Not only did Alexandra know how I felt, but she was telling me just the things I had been wanting to say to her. Nevertheless, there was no question that she had the upper hand now. With all our cards on the table, it was up to me to win the game.

I was looking at her in admiration, at the way her face changed from smiling to cunning to frowning. Without a doubt, I was very much in love with her and I was unable to disguise my desire. Looking at her naked splendor on the bed next to me, I felt like a pirate who's finally reached land after months at sea. I had to control myself.

She finished her coffee, jumped out of bed and said, "Com'n, time for the beach!"

A happy and dangerous day was beginning for me.

The terrace of Paraportiani, facing the open sea with the spread nets, was one of the places where I'd spend hours of thinking alone. Once I said that I wanted to build a grave below the base of the cliff, for me. Only that girl knew this secret because only her did I love so paranoiclly.

The waves crashed on to the foot of the cliff. On the same cliff my home was built in Venice.

Winter was beautiful in Mykonos.

The frothy waves caused by the winter north winds crashed onto the pier.

The rowboats hit the sea in both summer and winter to bring all kinds of merchandise back to the island. The most regular are those of Bonny and captain George of Mathoupe.

The wild winter waves brake onto the lonely beach.

Tasos' rowboat with spread out nets, far from the cape of coffee.

"The octopuses die standing". The drunkards traditional delicasy.

Much could happen, or nothing night happen. Marilena was far away; we had both put her out of our minds.

Along the way to the beach we stopped for breakfast. Alexandra had two eggs and bread with fresh butter and honey. She was famished after the strenuous night.

"Where are we going swimming today, Strati?" she asked me. From the next table, Tassos, the fisherman, suggested we all go together to Tragonisi to dive for crabs.

"Great, let's go!" Alexandra exclaimed joyously.

The three of us set out and stopped at Kiouka's cafeneion to find Nicolas, Tassos' apprentice. None of the fishermen who hang out there had seen the boy, so Tassos suggested we have our first ouzo while we waited for him to show up.

Kiouka's cafeneion is one of the last remnants of an era quickly fading away. It has no more than ten small tables with marble tops which Kioukas cleans with a sponge drenched in vinegar every time the customer changes. The walls are the most interesting sight in the place. There isn't an inch that isn't covered with every available variety of posters and photographs.

Ancient Greeks, beer ads and old movie posters were jumbled up among soccer players, record covers, deodorant ads and contemporary politicians.

"All of Greece is in here", Alexandra exclaimed as she looked around in amusement. Meanwhile, the second round of ouzo had arrived, and Tassos' apprentice was nowhere to be seen.

"Do you know what the guy playing backgammon at the corner table does for a living?" Tassos asked me.

"He's a travel agent, isn't he?"

"A travel agent, my eye!" Tassos said scornfully.

"Well, that's what the sign on his office says: Travel and

Emigration."

"Oh, forget about the sign on the door! He's an undertaker!"

"You mean he undertakes the migration of people to heaven."

"Yes, exactly!" Tassos replied.

"And where does he find enough dead people on the island!"

"He imports them."

"What are you talking about, you madman! He imports dead bodies?"

Tassos emptied his ouzo in one gulp, puffed on his cigarette, and started explaining how Dimitris makes a living by importang dead bodies.

"Have you seen the cruise ships carrying all those people every summer?" he asked.

"Of course", I answered.

"What kind of people are on them?"

"What do you mean what kind. People! Tourists!"

"Have you ever noticed their age?"

"Well, they're not too young", I answered, realizing what he was driving at.

"Not too young! The youngest one is sixtyfive! They're living corpses. And they die!" he added triumphantly and ordered a third round of ouzo. Just then Nicolos, the apprentice, walked in.

"Drink up. It's time to go!" Tassos said and got up, emptying his glass. "I'll finish the story in the caique.

I started to pay, but meanwhile Tassos had already done so, having bought two bottles for the road.

We left the cafeneion and headed for the little dock where Tassos had his caique.

It was freshly painted a bright sky blue heat and furry

equipped. The apprentice started the engine and we were off. There was a soft breeze coming from the island of Tinos. The sea was a deep blue and the sun was hot enough to warm us from the light wind. I looked at Alexandra, a vision among the colours and the feelings of joy and tranquility. The ouzo had had its affects on all of us.

"Paradise isn't fenced in", Tassos contemplated. "Anyone can walk in freely."

"Joy without boundaries", Alexandra added, looking at me with a meaningful smile.

Yes, this was heaven - staring at the froth on either side, embraced by the sun, cooled off by the breeze. After having brought out the first bottle of ouzo and an octupus dried in the sun, Tassos was softly playing his bouzouki and humming.

Alexandra was sitting across from me, facing the open sea; as I was looking at her, the land in the background seemed to be bobbing up and down behind her head, to the rhythm of the caique.

Infinity seemed to be captured in her eyes, just as it was captured in the sea she was gazing at. I couldn't take my eyes off her and, in order to break the spell, she refilled our glasses and asked Tassos to finish his story about the importation of dead bodies.

"There are about twenty cruise ships", Tassos picked up the thread of his story, "which take thousands of people to the islands every year. Nearly all of them, as we already said, are on their last voyage before departing for another, more peaceful world. They want to go happy, with their tired lungs full of fresh sea air. But many of them - either because of the change of climate, or because they're seasick, or because of plain old age - never make the round trip. So someone dies in the boat - what's the captain going to do? He can't very well throw him into the sea, because his relatives are bound to start looking for the body. So he shoves the body into the refrigerator where meat is kept - that way the stench doesn't reach the other passengers.

"Meanwhile, he's got to get rid of the body - there's no reason to let it continue a cruise it can no longer enjoy. so what does he do?

"He simply sends word to Dimitris - the "travel agent" - that there's merchandise in the fridge for him. The captain arranges a late stop at Mykonos, so Dimitris can take a launch in the dark and load the body onto it, under the fruit and vegetables.

"Being frozen, the body lasts a day or two, so Dimitris takes it to a little church where the priest is in on the deal. A service is conducted, to defreeze the poor man's soul before he's buried. Then Erato, Dimitris' wife enters the scene, to hold an all-night dirge. The next day he's buried. Dimitris has arranged everything - even the cemetary's watchman is in the business, having allotted a space where Dimitris throws all the bodies."

Tassos took a sip of ouzo and went on:

"Now here's how the deal works: after the burial, Dimitris sends for Susan - the American painter, you know her - and for fifty drachmas (painters have to make a living, after all) Susan writers the letter and lists the funeral expenses in English. The letter usually goes something like this:

"Mrs. Gertrude Smith, widow of John Smith
Alabama - U.S.A.

With great grief I inform you that as of a few days ago your dear husband is no longer among the living. Now

84

that you're alone in the world, it might console you to know that it was a good thing God rested his soul - he looked tortured even as a corpse.

Try to recover quickly, and when you do, please send me a check for the following expenses which I made on your behalf:

Drs. 1500 - launche to and from the cruise ship to load the body

" 1000 - transfer of body from the dock to church

" 800 - priest's expenses for funeral service

" 1000 - all-night dirge

" 500 - taverna expenses (We took him there before the burial to cool off his soul with some ouzo) ....

"At this point", Tassos went on, "the bastard adds various odd expenses for the grave, etc., and brings the total cost to 10,000 drs. adding that he can arrange for a memorial service for an additional 3,000."

"So that's how Dimitris makes money", Tassos concluded with a look of disgust on his face. It was too much for his seaman's temperament that anyone could make a business of other people's sorrow.

By now, Tragonisi - "Goat's Island - was clearly in view. Tassos knew the area well and steered the boat towards the caves with the crabs and lobsters.

Alexandra smiled, looking carefree and content. The mood was contagious, for I, too, felt that way now. The agony and the problems of yesterday seemed far, far away. As for Marilena, it was as if she had never existed.

We had reached the island and Tassos anchored by the opening of the big cave. The water was crystal clear; high cliffs rose on either side of the cave. Alexandra and I were enraptured by the scene. More practical, Tassos had already made his first dive underwater and came up with a crab: "Just a sample", he explained.

The second time he stayed underwater longer and came up with an enormous lobster which beat itself wildly against the deck until Nicolos quick and skillful hands gave it the final blow. He threw it into a pot of sea water.

After a few more dives, Tassos came up to rest.

"Get ready", he said to Alexandra. We're going down together next time.

He drank another ouzo to warm up from the freezing depths of the sea and started the pot boiling, it was already filling up with various kinds of fish. Then he started explaining to Alexandra what she was to do once they got under water. She listened carefully, trying to assimilate every detail. When Tassos had relaxed, they dived together and came up after a few minutes, Alexandra holding a little crab like a trophy. She was jumping up and down like a delighted little girl and Tassos congratulated her on her accomplishment.

They went down again several times, always bringing up some sort of catch. After a while Alexandra came up shivering from the cold waters. I gave her a towel to dry up, but instead she threw it on her back and came up to me. She put her arms around me, still shivering. Her body was wet and cold against mine. She held me tighter and tighter, whispering, "How nice and warm you are!" Dizzy with surprise and excitement, I tried to dry her back with the towel. Her whole body was glued against mine. Her trembling had stopped and she sighed contentedly. There was no doubt left in my mind - I was definitely not just a

86

"heater" for her.

We stayed like that for a few minutes. Softly she drew her face up to mine. Looking intently into my eyes, she brought her lips to mine. Her cool lips were soon bruning and she kissed me with a passion that made me feel I was melting. It was as if she was trying to wipe away all the anguish she had caused.

The funny thing was that I was the first to break the hold - either because I couldn't take it any longer, or because by now Tassos and Nicolos were both back on the boat.

The soup was ready, and Nicolos served it into four deep plates. Pieces of crab, moray and scorpion were swimming in it; it was abolutely delicious. Everything seemed miraculously good! The sun, the sea, the embraces, the soup! Yes, the soup was part of the sensual joy of the day.

The second bottle of ouzo was gone even before the food. Satisfied and tired, we set up a tent on the beach and lay down next to one another. Alexandra snuggled up close to me and fell asleep nestled in my arms.

It was late in the afternoon when Nicolas awakened with the strong aroma of coffee brewing. We drank it in silence, feeling calm and peaceful as the sea. The sun was leaning westward and had a glowing red color.

"I feel wonderful!" Alexandra exclaimed.

"It's the natural life", Nicolas smiled at her and cleaned up the coffee cups.

"Let's go back late, with the moonlight", she proposed.

"I have a better idea", Tassos intercepted. "When the sun is down, we'll go to St. Anna's, behind the Cape of Coffee. Tonight there's a hog slaying at Michalis the Wolf's house."

"What's that?" Alexandra asked him.

"Patience, you'll see ... There'll be music, too."

"You mean a feast? Alexandra insisted.

"No, silly. You've always got feasts on your mind! Tassos kidded her. Alexandra laughed like a little girl waiting for a surprise. She had changed totally since morning; the harshness on her face had been replaced by a look of peace and joy.

"Don't pick on the girl, Tasso", I said protectively and kissed her on the cheek.

She took my face in both her hands and gave me a quick, friendly kiss on the lips, as if to thank me for being on her side.

The sun was resting on the sea now and Nicolas was helping Tassos close up the tent before he started the engine going.

The cave's mouth looked black now; the crabs that had survived our invasion could rest for the night.

I mentioned to Tassos to let Alexandra take the helm. A thousand dreams passed before my eyes, as I watched her steering the boat like an amused child.

My wildest dreams were coming true. Tonight we would sleep together and my joy would be complete. And then what? Where is all this leading? It's too early to think about that, I told myself. I'd never been conservative in love, so why should I start now? I'd never been conservative in anything, come to think of it.

No, I wouldn't let anything disturb my happiness, reached after such misery and anguish. It was all mine to enjoy now. I had wanted Alexandra and I had her, and tonight I would have her in the actual sense of the word. I didn't care where it would lead. That's the way I was and I'd be that way now, too. I'd always done what pleased me.

I sprang up, angry at myself, and poured a glass of ouzo.

"That's right", Tassos said. "Get the demon inside you drunk so he'll leave you alone." He held out his glass to be filled.

Alexandra, still at the helm, saw us and asked with a hurt look: "Doesn't the captain deserve any?

Tassos filled a third glass and handed it to her. She took a sip and laughed:

"Here we go again!"

Yes, that was our life on the island. Fishing, drinking, being carefree. Tassos took over the helm as we were approaching the cape. We got into the little harbor of St. Anna and tied the boat to a big rock that stuck out of the water like a natural jetty. We put on a pair of shorts and a shirt and jumped out. Tasso, who knew the way to the house, walked ahead of us.

We had walked about two hundred metres, one behind the other on the narrow path, when we reached the little church. Behind it, another hundred metres away, was Michalis' house. Outside, an enormous pot of water was boiling over a glowing fire. We were greeted by the villagers who, before we knew it, had placed glasses of wine in our hands.

We had arrived just in time: the water with which the hog would be scalded was ready. Every year, when fall sets in, every village family slays a hog, with which it gets by most of the winter. The fat gives them lard; the entrails become sausages; the meat is kept in vinegar.

We sat around the fire, drinking our wine. The enormous hog was lying a few metres away, motionless, with a strange, sad look in its eye, as if he knew that all these people were rejoicing its death. Michalis asked his wife if everything was ready for the slaying. She took a look at the boiling water and answered yes. With heavy movements, Michalis got up. He was a tall, strong man with a big, curling grey mustache. He went into the kitchen and came out holding a small, sharp knife. He shoved it into his belt and looked at his brother, Athanas, who emptied his glass and got up. The atmosphere was heavy with the air of oncoming death.

I looked at Alexandra. Her eyes were wide in terror.

The two men were standing over the hog now. It let out a piercing moan and tried to get up.

"Now" Michalis yelled and leaped at the animal.

With a quick movement he grabbed its mouth in his left hand and held it shut. The animal moaned in agony, trying to get away, but Michalis' strong hand had clutched its mouth like a pair of pliers. His right hand was holding its front leg, trying to break it. It was a heavy animal, fighting for its life, that could cause pandemonium if it got away.

Meanwhile Athanas had grabbed its hind legs. Together, quick as lightning, the two brothers turned the pig over. It was wriggling wildly, but the hands of the "wolves" out did its strength. Michalis stamped his leg on its belly with force.

Alexandra had glued herself onto me and was holding onto my arm with both her hands. Her nails were tearing into my flesh, but it didn't hurt. I was too carried away by the sight of death before me.

Now Michalis let go of the hog's leg and pulled the knife from his belt. The blade glistened in the dark; we sat back watching in terror. I don't know if the animal saw the knife, perhaps it was instinct that made it writhe in utter agony. Alexandra pulled me even closer.

Still holding onto its mouth, Michalis shoved the knife into the throat of the giant animal. Blood spattered all over him and the animal moaned in pain, stretching out its body. A death rattle, together with blood and froth, escaped from its throat and then it collapsed. Blood was running from its nostrils, but the animal was already dead.

Michalis got up and sighed in relief. He looked wild. Two beasts had struggled and one had won.

Several men got up and hung the hog by its legs from a hook over the door. Its head leaned backwards and the slit in its throat got bigger and bigger.

The women were throwing boiling water over it, to help shed the hairs from its skin. Meanwhile the organs had started playing and the wine was running freely down our throats, dried up from the agony.

When the scalding was over, Michalis took the same knife, still drenched in blood, and ran it down the hog's middle, from its neck to its legs. Its insides spattered out, still hot with the life they held just a few minutes ago.

On a grill that had replaced the pot of water, Michalis threw pieces of the animal's entrails. The women then turned them over so they would grill evenly. Cautiously, Alexandra took piece of the well-cooked liver. The wine helped her forget the animal when it was alive and enjoy, instead, how good it tasted dead.

Meanwhile, others had come from the neighboring farmhouses, joining in the celebration. The music was getting louder, the wine was threatening to run out, the drunken reverly was growing more intense.

A cool autumn morning was approaching. Summer was gone and the sun took time before it began to warm us. Tired from the all-night merrymaking, Alexandra was leaning on my shoulder, half-asleep. Michalis' wife, Anousso, saw her and took her into the house to rest. Taking out two beautifully embroidered sheets from the chest that held her daughter's dowry, the woman made the bed where Alexandra would lie.

This wasn't a house where couples not united in marriage could sleep together, so I lay down with the other men, all in a row under the trees.

It was early afternoon when I woke up to the smell of coffee. Alexandra was already up and was holding up the yarn being wound by Michalis' mother. As soon as she saw me, she asked with a sly wink: "Did you sleep well? Isn't it funny, the way things happened? Again we slept in different beds!"

We drank our coffee and went for a walk around the farm. Alexandra was like a city child enjoying the beauty of the outdoors for the first time. We walked hand in hand, like any couple in love. No-one would have believed Alexandra was a girl with sexual perversions, looking at her next to me. The scheming, cunning look in her eyes was gone .. the look she had with Marilena. Marilena. Fleetingly, I wondered whatever had happened to her ... it all seemed so long ago.

We had been walking for quite a while, not saying a word, wrapped up in our own thoughts. It was just over a day since Marilena had left, and already I was looking at life anew.

I was pointing out to her the things that had real meaning in my life: the sea, the sun, the villagers, the caiques, the fishermen. Everything beautiful about the simple life with all the glory of its traditions. Enthusiastically, she agreed with me, looking fascinated, amused and frightened by them all at once.

When we got back to the house we had a bite to eat. The weather had been bad all day, but with the setting of the sun we expected the sea to quiet down so we could return. After saying goodbyes all around, we headed for the harbor where Tassos was waiting for us.

"Time to go", he called out. "By the time we're out, the sea will be calmer." The sun was setting behind the clouds by this time, but the waves were still big enough to rock the boat to and fro.

Alexandra looked a bit frightened and I gave her some ouzo to relax her nerves and poured some for myself and Tassos as well. "Tell her not to be afraid", Tassos said as I handed him the glass. "Old man Death doesn't want her yet - only you want her now, and she knows it. Be careful!"

A wise man, captain Tassos. He knew women well, like he knew the sea which, true to his predictions, was growing quieter. Soon we were entering the harbor. We'd been gone less than two days, and I felt like it had been a month.

We thanked Tassos, who gave us a lobster to grill for dinner and we headed for the house. We were almost there, when Alexandra turned and asked me uneasily:

"Do you suppose Marilena is back?"

Both her tone and her question were incomprehensible to me. Was she afraid of Marilena's possible return? Did she prefer to be alone with me? Or was she anxious to see her? I didn't think so, so I answered:

"Well, good for her if she's back!"

She turned to me with an innocent smile:

Are you always so cynical when you're no longer interested in someone?"

"I don't think I was ever interested in her", I answered

and meant it.

"But she was interested in you, and you know it!"

"You're going to call me cynical again, but the answer to that is that it's her problem!"

"Allright, allright, let's not make a fuss over whose problem it is. Only time will show."

Her words turned out to be almost prophetic, as things worked out. They imprinted themselves on my mind.

In the meantime we had reached the house and, even though I hated to admit it, I was more anxious than Alexandra. It didn't make any difference that I felt I had won the game; the fact was, that Marilena's appearance would have stood in my way.

I reached under the window sill and was relieved to find the key still there, where I had left it. Alexandra was looking at my hand, then raised her eyes to mine. She started to smile but changed her mind - this was no time for meaningless smiles; we both knew what was going to happen.

Without Marilena around, there would be no obstacles. Nevertheless, I knew that a long and difficult road lay ahead and I didn't even know where it led.

For the first time I entered the house with the quivering expectation of a schoolboy. At times like these, only humor can save the situation Heads or tails, I called out, to see who takes a bath first.

We hadn't washed in two days and we were both full of salt.

"Tails", Alexandra chose and won. I had to keep my word, even if I didn't like it. I lay down on the sofa and waited for her to finish her bath.

"What are we doing tonight?" she asked when she came out.

"Are you asking to see what you'll wear", I asked her sarcastically. "Not exactly", she said, "but one never knows with you. We might go out to dinner and end up sleeping on the marbles of Delos!"

She had come out of the bathroom half wet, with a towel wrapped around her luscious body.

"If you don't like it, find yourself a clerk so your life will be quiet and planned", I snapped at her.

"I'm glad to see your humor hasn't left you' she said sweetly and gave me a quick kiss on the cheek.

I took my bath while she got dressed and we went out feeling fresh and revived.

"I feel like going on the town tonight", she announced. "We've had enough of feasts and hog slayings. I'm beginning to feel like a hilibilly with you!"

We were near the "Monte Parnasse" bar by now and I suggested we have our first drink there. "The atmosphere is just what you need", I told her.

Manolis, the owner, has created an atmosphere that is unique, beginning with the music. If the composers of the music he plays were alive, the youngest one would be a hundred and eighty! He was playing wagner's "Tristan and Izolde" when we walked in and only when I asked for something a bit lighter did he reluctantly change it to a Tchaikovsky concert.

The walls were full of posters but not of the variety in Kiouka's cafeneion - no politicians, no slogans, no modern movie stars. Here, the enormous behind of Toulouze-Lautrec's heroine reigned in all its splendor, keeping good company with Edith Piaf and Maurice Chevalier in his famous top hat. All of them dead, I thought, and finished my vodka. There had been too much death around for the past few days, so I suggested we have the next drink in a gayer atmosphere.

We had a few more drinks at another bar and then went for dinner to a seaside restaurant. We ordered hors d'oevres and meanwhile I sent a boy home to bring the lobster Tassos had given us. We made small talk over dinner and then fell silent. We were each trying to guess what was on the other's mind, although the answer was obvious.

I was drinking to chase away the intense feeling of expectation and desire that was driving me crazy. Alexandra effected me so strongly, that I was afraid of the day after the night of love I'd been waiting for so long.

Angry at myself for being so childish, I got up without having finished the lobster.

"Where are you heading for" she asked sarcastically.

"Nowhere in particular. I'm just not hungry any more." This girl was always a step ahead of me, I thought. She was making me a nervous wreck.

We got up and headed towards the house. On the way we stopped at the "Monte Parnasse" again, where I gulped down a double vodka.

"You're acting as if you're about to jump without a parachute", she remarked, "and drinking to summon up your courage!"

She was really getting on my nerves. I decided to strike back: "I don't need courage, I just don't particularly feel like jumping!"

We walked home in silence, feeling the coldness that had so suddenly developed between us. We went each to our room, without even saying goodnight. Absent-mindedly I undressed and got into bed.

The moon was shining into the room and I lay there, staring at the shadows on the ceiling and thinking about

The octapus needs a lot of work before it's thrown onto the fire.

Paragios was hitting the octapus so it could soften before it was put on the charcoal to eat.

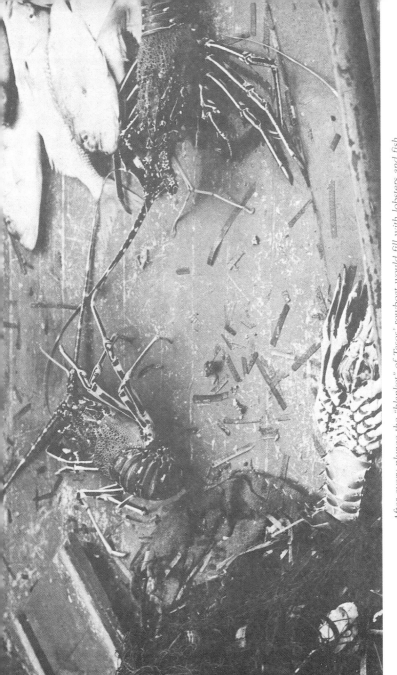

After every plunge the "blanket" of Tasos' rowboat would fill with lobsters and fish.

The beach of Psarou, during a period of summer happiness.

We'd go to Elia and Calamopodi that were long beaches, by boat and return late in the afternoon, enjoying a magical journey with the sunset.

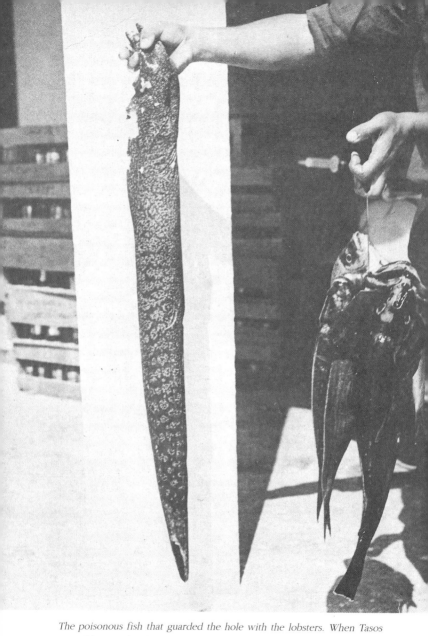

The poisonous fish that guarded the hole with the lobsters. When Tasos lifted it after he cut its throat with a harpoon we all shivered.

*Even sitting by the shore, the sea always scared Marilena. She always
had a bad instinct about nature.*

Unlike Alexandra she loved the air and everything else that the island offered her.

the sudden change that had taken place. For forty-eight hours I had been in heaven. For forty-eight hours I had tried to reach a certain point and I had succeeded. What had suddenly come over me? Now that I was about to have this girl I wanted and loved so, one word had destroyed everything.

As these thoughts were passing through my mind and I was trying to figure out how I could smooth things out, I became aware of Alexandra's shadow entering the room.

"I came to say goodbye", she said and my blood froze. She was still dressed and had her bag thrown over her shoulder. I sat up and, unable to hide my anguish, I mumbled: "Where are you going?"

"Back to my old room".

Trying to control myself, I asked her: "At this time of night?"

"It's better this way, Strati", she answered. "I don't like it when the people I feel something for drink so they won't remember anything the next day."

I could do one of two things now: either say, "So long, if that's the way you want it", in which case she would almost certainly leave, or I could try to explain my actions. I didn't have the courage to try the first way, but my ego wouldn't let me act otherwise.

"Allright", I said calmly, "if that's what you want. But people who feel something, as you said, don't throw it out so easily."

She hesitated for a minute. Then she sat on the edge of the bed and just looked at me without saying a word. She had to make a decision. I didn't dare say anything; it was a crucial moment.

After what seemed an eternity, she got up slowly. Her mind was made up. She went towards the terrace, then abruptly turned around and started to undress. She threw off the shirt and the jeans she was wearing. Standing in the moonlight, nude and with a wild look in her eyes, she looked nothing like the girl on the nudist beach. She was a woman now, a woman with a splendid body, full of passion, ready to attack and be attacked.

She came into my bed. Her whole body was burning, her breathing was irregular. I took her face in both my hands and kissed her, unable to stop. I kissed her eyes, her nose, her lips, feeling something I had never even come close to experiencing before. It was a night unlike any other, a night full of love and endless passion.

The moon was leaving the room. Daylight was approaching. Unaware of anything but ourselves, we made love endlessly, passionately, as if each time were the first.

Sunlight was entering the room. Worn out, we fell into a blissful sleep locked in each other's arms.

CHAPTER 16

The room was hot when I woke up. It must have been past noon. Alexandra was in a deep sleep, half her body on mine and the other half almost out of the bed.

Her long black hair almost reached the floor. I wanted to get up but was afraid of disturbing her. Just then I happened to look across the room and my gaze stopped at Marilena's bed. I felt as if an electric current had run through my body. The bed had been slept in. And yet, no-one had slept here, unless ... And then I saw Marilena's little suitcase under the bed.

Now I sprang up for good. The feeling of guilt was overwhelming. Alexandra snuggled close to me and with her eyes half-closed, she went to kiss me.

"Marilena", I said and my voice betrayed how helpless I felt.

She opened her eyes wide.

"Where is she?" she asked in a frightened voice.

I showed her the bed. "She must have slept here", I said in a whisper.

"What!" she shrieked and jumped out of bed. She was pale, almost chalk white. She ran out of the room and started looking for her. Marilena was nowhere to be found. She came back into the room, still with the same colour on her face. She sat on the bed.

"Where could she be now?" she asked in a small voice.

"I don't know where she is now, but she was obviously in her bed last night".

I pointed toward the bed again. "She must have been sleeping when I came in last night", I went on.

"And you didn't see her! she screamed.

"I didn't turn the light on. I got straight into bed".

"You mean she was here all night, right in this room! she whispered desperately.

"She must have seen everything", I agreed helplessly.

"It's not possible!" she stammered with a look of agony on her face.

"Do you know how long she's been in love with you?"

I listened without speaking, my feelings of guilt getting stronger.

"When you asked her to join you in Mykonos", Alexandra went on, "her life's dream was coming true."

"And since when have I been someone's life dream?"

"Cut out the wise cracks. This is no time to be funny!" she scolded me and continued, "When here in Mykonos you were still indifferent towards her and wouldn't make love to her, I found her that night at Billy's bar, looking miserable and drinking to forget you. Marilena is a very sensitive girl. She realized that since even here, living in the same room with you, nothing was happening, her game would be lost for good in Athens. I don't know what she would have done that night if I hadn't talked to her, listened to her problems. She needed someone badly that night ..."

"And that was the chance you were waiting for ..."

"Stop being vulgar!" She spat out at me, her black eyes aglow. "The night she came into my room, she came because she couldn't stand being in the same room with you any longer! She couldn't stand having you next to her and ignoring her completely! I induced her to make love with me. She had never been with a woman before, and she had no other choice with what you were doing to her."

"People shouldn't let others make choices for them. They should have the strength to control their feelings."

"Well, she didn't" Alexandra yelled frantically. "What do you want now?"

"You're yelling to defend yourself, so I won't reproach you for what you did! I retorted.

"I already told you: she had no other choice. She thought maybe you would get jealous and react. But you ... once again, you only thought of yourself."

"While you thought of her well-being, I suppose?"

"I didn't deny anything, but I still think you're the one who's responsible for this modern tragedy!"

"I think it would be a good idea to stop accusing each other and to figure out how we're going to face her now."

"I have nothing to face!" she screamed in a rage. "You're going to face everything! Alone!"

She was hysterical now and went on:

"You're responsible, it's all your doing, you're the guilty one! I'm leaving! I'm leaving this house, leaving this island!"

She slammed the door behind her and went to the terrace for some air. The entire situation was unbearable. Could it be that I would lose Alexandra and then have to face Marilena in all her tragic glory? I couldn't take it. I went out to the terrace and found her leaning on the wooden railing, looking vacantly at the sea. I went near her and put my arms around her waist.

"I'm leaving", she repeated, but in a more relaxed tone.

"You're not going anywhere" I said with finality and

went on, "I have no reason to make amends to anyone. I did nothing to give me a guilty conscience."

"You have no conscience" she snapped back.

"Well, then, you aren't going to give me one and neither is Marilena", I answered and moved away from her. After a few seconds I went on in a firm and quiet tone:

"Listen, Alexandra. There's no point in arguing over who's guilty and who's not. Life goes on. Com'n, go get your things and we'll go to the beach. We'll probably run into her somewhere."

She listened to me without saying a word and then went to her room to get ready. We left the house and got on a boat for St. Stephanos beach. The weather was pleasant, with a light breeze that was refreshing in the hot sun. I felt great - and why not? I had spent the most beautiful night I can remember. I really was in love with Alexandra and after having made love with her, in the way that we did, all night, my love had grown even stronger.

Unfortunately, I didn't think she felt the same. She was silent and gloomy. She looked intently at the sea, as the little boat was rocking up and down in the waves. Being a woman, she was more sensitive to Marilena's feelings. Certainly she would have preferred to spare her friend the sight of us in bed last night. Perhaphs she felt remorse - and now that Marilena was back, whatever Alexandra had felt for her might be rekindled.

Suddenly a thought passed through my mind: maybe she regretted what had happened last night! No matter that she looked happy at the time - that was before Marilena's unexpected return.

I was back where I had started. Marilena's presence brought back the torture and the uncertainly of the past. Why had she come back?

I offered her a cigarette to see how she would react, hoping that she would prove it was just my sick imagination acting up again. But no, she didn't take it. She shook her head without even looking at me. She wasn't just absent-minded; the same thoughts were running through her head and she was trying to make a decision.

When we reached the beach we headed straight for the little cafeneion on the hill, from where we could see the entire stretch of white sandy beach. There were few people. Without realizing it, my eyes scanned the beach for Marilena. I knew this was her favorite spot and she had occasionally come alone because it was the closest to town. Marilena wasn't there.

I ordered ouzo for Alexandra and myself, and as I turned to hand her the glass I noticed a lone figure walking along a small stretch of beach hidden between two enormous rocks. It was Marilena. I shoved Alexandra:

"Your friend is meditating", I said with a touch of sarcasm.

She turned in the direction I was pointing and got up abruptly.

"I'll go talk to her".

I took her hand and pulled her down again.

"Drink your ouzo first and don't get nervous!"

But meanwhile I was also upset. Marilena's return had created problems for both of us. She was a rival that wouldn't leave me in peace with the girl I loved.

Alexandra sipped a little ouzo and got up again. She went down the hill towards the bay and approached Marilena. They stood facing each other for a minute. Alexandra was the first to take a step forward, and then they ran into each other's arms. They stayed that way for what seemed an eternity to me. Then they took each other's hand and started walking up and down. Marilena seemed to be doing all the talking.

This turn of events didn't please me a bit. I ordered another ouzo and wandered in agony what Alexander would do. Would she stay with me or would she, either out of love or pity, return to Marilena?

This time things were worse for me than before. Now I knew how much I loved Alexandra. I had won her, she had become mine, and yet I had to try to get her back again. From the look on her face, Alexandra didn't seem to have reached a decision yet. What would she do? Would she sleep with me one day and with Marilena the next? I didn't think I could bear that; it would be better for me to leave. But could I find the strength? I had started to doubt everything. I felt like a schoolboy who hasn't done his homework again.

I couldn't take it any longer. I was tired of trying to persuade Alexandra that she should stay with me. If only Marilena had stayed in Athens! What the hell had gotten into her? I was so worked up that I felt like throwing her down the hill when she got close to me! She was ruining my life again!

I realized I was too much of an egotist - but why not? I had always done as I pleased, and now this little pipsqueak was getting the better of me!

The girls had reached my table, but I couldn't muster up a show of joy at seeing her. I just asked her about her brother and she said he was doing fine. Then I went down for a swim. The cold water would do me good, I thought. After all, don't cold showers always calm people down? I managed to laugh at my predicament and went to lie in the sun. After some time, the girls called me up for lunch.

The food was good, the drink helped me forget my worries and the day was a pleasant one. But autumn had set in for good, and by about four o'clock it started getting chilly. We got up to leave.

CHAPTER 17

I got straight into bed as soon as we returned home. I had no intention of missing my afternoon siesta with my troubled thoughts. The girls stayed in the living room to chat.

I woke up in the early evening. No-one was home. Everything was quiet. I walked out to the terrace and faced a calm sea and the sun setting behind the mountains.

"Here we go again", I thought to myself. Now that Marilena was back, Alexandra would be with her most of the time and I would have to start wandering around the island again, looking for them. Sick and tired of the whole situation, I went into the bathroom. Bright red lipstick informed me from the mirror: "Ten o'clock at Fouskis for dinner." No signature, and I couldn't tell which one the handwriting belonged to - not that it made any difference at this point.

I was beginning to feel like an innkeeper, who had a picturesque house with a unique view towards the sea to offer and good service, in the form of my maid Maria.

As for meals, well, all my guests had to do was leave orders as to when and where I should offer them. Wonderful! Moreover, if one of the ladies were in need of sexual satisfaction, I was always available to offer it.

Maybe it seems exaggerated, but that's the way I felt

and I wasn't at all proud of myself. I walked out of the house and along the harbor. On the way I ran into my old friend Dimitris standing outside his tourist shop.

"Hey, Strati! What are you looking for wandering around like that?"

"I'm not looking for anything. What are you doing?"

"I'm fishing for customers, as usual, but you've already got yours! What did you do with your duplex tonight?"

I was in no mood for jokes and, in any case, anytime someone referred to the girls it annoyed me. I smiled without answering and went on.

His comments made me start thinking about my reputation on the island. They must have been gossiping about my strange situation and it worried me, because the islanders were my friends and we drank and had fun together, but never before had they kidded me about my private life.

I didn't like it, but there was nothing I could do about it. Putting an end to the whole situation didn't even cross my mind. For two days and two nights I had been in heaven with Alexandra, and now Marilena came and everything was gone. People noticed these things, just as people had obviously noticed that I was crazy about Alexandra.

I had reached Alecos' bar by this time. Its dim lights revealed only a few shadows at one table. I sat at the bar and ordered a scotch. All the pessimistic thoughts going around in my head must have affected the colour on my face, because Alecos asked me what was the matter in a way I found strange. I answered drily that nothing was wrong and went to pay for the drink. "It's on the house", Alecos said, "maybe I can help chase away the evil spirits."

I walked out feeling even worse. Things were geeting

out of control, or so I imagined. It was no longer a personal issue between me and the girls - it had become an item of interest for the entire island.

I realized I was getting panickly, but I couldn't help it. My self-control was fighting with my desperate desire for Alexandra. I had to straighten myself out to see what could be done.

I reached Fouski's restaurant before ten, the time at which I had been asked to appear. I ordered a bottle of wine and something to nibble on while I was waiting. Trying not to think about the same things over and over again, I sat listening intently to the music.

Fouskis came toward me, his glass in hand, and sat down.

"Hey, what's the matter?" he asked.

Here we go again, I thought. Everyone is making fun of me.

"Nothing! Should something be the matter?"

"Oh, come'n! You sit there alone, you don't talk to anyone, and you look like the widow of the unknown soldier!"

I burst out laughing, because Fouskis always found the right expression to describe something. And, after all, he was my friend and had a right to ask.

"I don't think it's anything specific", I answered.

"Specific or not, you look miserable and mixed-up! I'm not used to you that way! I don't know what those two do between themselves, but I suppose you've had your fun with whichever one you like. Right?"

"Right", I said nodding my head.

"Fine! So what's bothering you? You don't talk to a soul anymore!"

"I really don't think it's that bad", I said trying to look

cheerful. "Maybe you don't think so, but I do because I can see more clearly from a distance. And since you don't want to tell me what it is, I'll tell you what I think. If you're an honest man, admit that I'm right!"

He filled his wine glass and started:

"You're not the worrying kind." "You have your fun and don't give a damn! So what's bothering you about those two?" I started to answer but he took my hand and stopped me.

"It's your egotism", he went on. "You think to yourself: I should be enough for her. Why should she go with the girl, since she's with me?" But why do you take it that way, instead of just having your fun, like you've done all your life?"

He looked at me searchingly and waited for an answer. I took a sip and very calmly answered:

"Because I love her and I don't want to share her with anyone."

He didn't seem to understand, or maybe it was just that he couldn't find an answer to my honest confession. Finally he started to say something but didn't finish; the girls had smilingly come into the restaurant and greeted us.

Alexandra took my glass, made a toast and emptied it in one gulp. Fouskis got up and went into the kitchen; the girls sat on either side of me. Marilena was thoughful and didn't seem too happy by my presence. I doubted she realized how annoyed I was by hers!

Alexandra, on the other hand, was in a very good mood and that, together with the talk I'd had with Fouskis, helped cheer me up. Momentarily I thought of going to Athens for a few days for a change of scene but I wasn't sure yet.

Throughout dinner, Marilena remained silent. She, too, was obviously bothered by the way things had turned out. She, too, had an a ego. All around, it was evident that a solution to this crazy mix-up had to be found, but I couldn't see it coming. None of the three seemed ready to give in, even though I considered my position the clearest. Perhaps I should take a firm stand and insist Marilena leave the island. But could I be sure that Alexandra wouldn't leave with her? It was just another vicious circle!

Abruptly, Marilena got up and announced she was going to sleep. A strange mixture of feelings overtook me: joy at the thought that perhaps I would stay alone with Alexandra and anxiety that she might leave with Marilena. Before I could straighten out my emotions, the decision had been made. Alexandra jumped up and said:

"Wait! I'm coming with you!"

She was looking for her handbag on one of the chairs.

I don't know what made me react the way I did or whether it was the right thing to do. Nevertheless, I grabbed her arm and made her sit down again.

What a mistake! Alexandra wasn't the kind of woman who gives in to force. She softly took my hand from her arm and, with a sarcastic smile on her face, said:

"Don't play tough with me, Humphrey Bogart!"

Calmly, and still smiling sarcastically, she walked off after Marilena, who meanwhile had reached the door.

I was dumbfounded. My hands were trembling and the blood rushed wildly through my head. My mouth felt like the Sahara. I had lost all sense of time and space. I reached for the first full glass of wine before me and gulped it down.

My first reaction was: and now what? I felt helpless; bitterness had spread through my body like a thick black liquid. All my dreams - which last night had become reality - had crumbled so suddenly.

I couldn't take it any longer. How could a girl like Alexandra, no matter how beautiful, no matter how much I wanted her, reduce me to this? I had to react. But how? The fact that I was so madly in love with her left no room for logic.

The simplest thing to do, of course, was to pack up and go back to Athens; but that was out of the question. I got up and walked out of the restaurant without paying. I would take care of the bill tomorrow, because today it would be impossible to face Fouskis' inquisitive eyes. I walked along the narrow, empty streets, avoiding the crowded ones for fear I would run into someone.

I didn't even want to say hello to my friends. Passing by Pierro's bar I decided a drink would help. Pierro's is frequented mostly by foreigners, so there was less chance of meeting friends. Unfortunately, the bar was crowded tonight. I climbed on one of the few empty stools and ordered a scotch.

I don't know how many drinks later it was, when I heard a familiar phrase from a familiar voice:

"Dark thoughts are bad for you ..."

It was the same girl, who only a few days ago - the night I'd met Alexandra - had tried to comfort me with those words and a glass of champagne.

It was Jill, just back from a cruise around the Cyclades islands. She was in Mykonos for the night, before, sailing off for St. Topez.

"You're my lucky girl", I said sarcastically. "Every time I see you I'm just a step from suicide!"

Nonetheless, I was glad to see her. She told me about her cruise and she carried me with her around the islands.

111

At least by talking I got away from thinking about Alexandra. I felt almost grateful to her. Her carefree approach to life could barely touch me and my problems, but even that slight touch felt good. And, strangely enough, she showed a lively interest in me and my worries!

We drank together and talked for a long time and at some point went down to a table where another couple was sitting, the only passengers to remain on the yacht with Jill. The rest of her friends had flown back to Athens from Santorini.

When we reached the table Jill introduced me to her friends, a married couple in their thirties. They ordered another bottle of champagne which, after several whiskies, was just what I needed: Alexandra was now a hazy faraway shadow in my mind. When I realized I would have to go back to that miserable house to sleep in the room next to where they would be making love again, a thought flashed through my mind: I had no choice but to desert. I knew Jill would ask me to join her on the boat later on, and I started getting used to the idea.

When the last bottle of champagne was empty, there was no need for words. Her eyes extended the invitation; mine accepted.

We strolled towards the boat, her arm around my waist and mine around her shoulders. The cool breeze helped clear my dizzy head. When we reached the shiny black boat with the enormous white sails, I stopped and asked her:

What time is it?

"Three thirty", she answered with a hint of worry in her voice. It was several seconds before I spoke again:

"Let's go", I said decisively.

Marilena took pleasure in all the joys of the Mykonean sea.

There's no cooler caress than the sea of Mykonos.

.... and was always searching for something, Marilena.

From subconscious sense she always seemed to be awaiting something.

The sun's joy drawn on the people's carefree bodies.

On the beautiful seashores of Mykonos there's no sexual insufficiency or hungry glances.

This is Alexandra. The perfect creature, I madly fell in love with.

Even Alexandra's hair moved with sexual joy.

"Let's go where?" she wondered.

"Wake up the crew! Didn't you say you were leaving for St. Tropez in the morning? Well, this is the best time to start out!"

She stared at me in happy surprise. Happy because I would be going with her, surprise because she hadn't realized just how crazy I could be.

In ten minutes we were sailing off. The lights from the harbor were slowly fading away. The house' in "Venice" was easy to spot. There were lights on and I wondered what could be going on in my house. Suddenly I realized I was leaving Alexandra in this crazy way and I wished her she were lying next to me, like that glorious day on the caique!

Where am I going, I wondered, and who am I going with? Thankfully Jill came and sat next to me, forcing my eyes and my mind away from the lights in my house. By the time I looked back again, the lights had disappeared and only the black shadows of the cliffs were visible.

I was lying in Jill's arms now, staring at the myriads of stars above. When the sky is clear in Mykonos, the stars seem as close as the lights in the house next door ..... the sky seems within arm's reach from my favorite place in the world.

"Where' your mind wandering to, Don Quixote?"

I was surprised to hear that so familiar phrase from Jill. It was what Marilena used to ask me when I was absent-minded. What strange creatures women are! Jill and Marilena were literally day and night - and yet they found the same words to express the same feeling!

I was mixed up and angry, but Jill knew how to soothe me, stroking my head as she held me protectively in her arms.

113

CHAPTER 18

No matter how much a man resemble a beast, there are moments when he is tamed, if only to become a beast again at another time, another place, with other people.

Jill had tamed me. She was aware of my problem and knew how to handle it. With each moment that passed near her, Alexandra went more deeply into my subconscious. In time, only the lower back of my brain was still in love with her.

That first night on the boat she looked after me as if I were her child. I was in bad shape, and American women generally are good at mothering their men.

When I woke up late the next morning, we were sailing off the coast of Monemvasia. I hadn't suspected we weren't following the usual course until after I'd finished my coffee. The sea looked familiar and it definitely wasn't anywhere between Mykonos and Piraeus.

Not wanting to show my anxiety, I kiddingly asked Jill:

"Are we sailing the Pacific?"

"No! The southern Peloponnese", she answered indifferently.

I realized we were leaving Greece and knew it would look ridiculous if I tried to back out now.

"And why didn't we sail the Corinth Isthmus? Were you afraid I'd jump off?"

"I hadn't realized you were the boy dolphin", she

answered in a hurt tone.

"I think I'm more like Hemingway's "Old Man and the Sea", I added playfully.

"The captain had never sailed the Corinth gulf and didn't want to try it at night. In any case, he said it wouldn't take much longer what with all the delay at the Isthmus."

"Fine - so now would you tell me where you're planning to take me with just the pants I've got on and some change in my pocket?"

"We'll lend you both pants and change", she said sarcastically.

"Thanks a lot, but I still don't know where you're taking me!"

"What do you mean "where we're taking you?" Didn't we say, to St. Tropez?"

I thanked her for the information and had some more coffee, then went up on deck alone. A pleasant breeze was blowing up the enormous sails. The coast wasn't far off and the upright cliff of Monemvasia was clearly visible.

I was happy, but only on the surface. The air, the morning saltiness of the sea all around me, this beautiful vessel comprised the joys of my life. I'd never felt truly happy away from the sea; often I'd wondered how there was such a thing as mountain-climbers in the world!

Suddenly I realized that something was missing. I thought of Alexandra making coffee in my house and wondered what she might be thinking about my disappearance. Would the girls be worried? Surely they would soon start looking for me.

Even though I yearned to be back in Mykonos, I knew that the course I was following was the only one that might lead to success. At least Alexandra would feel guilty and worried about me. I smiled inwardly in satisfaction and yet I asked myself, why can't I get that girl off my mind. Maybe it was because she wasn't all mine - I could think up loads of excuses, but the fact remained.

"What's wrong this time?" I heard Jill asking.

"Myself," I answered.

She was holding a large glass of tomato juice in her hand and offerred me a sip. It turned out not to be quite as pure and healthy as it looked - the tomato juice had been added for colour and taste; the rest was vodka.

"You start out pretty early around here, don't you?" I asked her with a smile.

Soon I had an enormous glass all to myself, and as I sat there sipping on the drink I realized it was time to find out something about my hostess. After all, I was at her mercy in this luxurious vessel, which I also knew nothing about. I remembered that a film director friend of mine had once remarked that a yacht is the perfect place for a chic murder.

The colour of my drink and the name itself - Bloody Mary - made me even warier of my surroundings, but after an hour of listening to bits and pieces from Jill's life, it became clear that my imagination had gone too far. She was simply yet another rich, spoiled American girl, the kind whose daddy had made a fortune during prohibition and had thus been born in wealth and luxury - the kind that comprise American high society.

The yacht, I learned, was returning to St. Tropez to spend the winter, while its twin was awaiting Jill in Miami for her strolls in the Caribean.

Surely it was strange that with her looks and money Jill was alone in Mykonos, and stranger still that I happened to wind up in her net. She had been a godsend for me in my misery; from what I gathered there had been a Bob somewhere along the way who for some reason had disembarked at one of the ports. He might be waiting for her - for us, rather - in St. Tropez, but that would be his problem.

The first day at sea drifted pleasantly into a soft night. The wind was down and so we started the engines going. Soon we would be sailing north towards Sicily.

The night was beautiful and the moon, the same one that last night had been lighting up my windows in "Venice", appeared in all its glory.

Even if I had really wanted to forget Alexandra, there she was before me, like an astronaut in the night. I sat and stared at the moon with longing, almost as if Alexandra dwelled on its silvery surface. Without a doubt, she continued to exist, or at least co-exist, in my new, carefree world. Once more I knew that for sure she was something important in my life.

Thankfully, a divine instinct seemed to take over Jill whenever I lapsed into one of my moody sessions. There she was again now:

"Does the sea make you romatic?"

What could I answer? On such a night, with such a moon, on such a yacht, even the Boston Strangler would have become romantic! "It's not the sea", I answered pulling her close to me. "Unfortunately, I'm romantic by nature!"

"Don't say it's unfortunate!" she replied. "If only you knew how many people would like to be that way and can't! God has made only a chosen few romantic, while so many spend their life in a way that seems attractive on the surface, but there's nothing beneath. Nothing would seem important in life, if we weren't romantic and sensitive. You

117

wouldn't be here now, we wouldn't have been sailing towards St. Tropez, none of all this would have happened if we weren't a touch romantic ..."

It was the first time I had become engaged in such a conversation with Jill, and it was a pleasant surprise. Our conversation lasted for hours and revealed many new facets of Jill's personality to me, and this in turn made her more and more likeable. Every so often the steward filled our glasses with champagne and, as evening turned to night, I knew that Jill had conquered me. What had started as a get away from Alexandra had turned into a new, American-style happiness at sea.

It was time for dinner and the others came up on deck. I had hardly noticed their presence until now. They seemed very compatible, in a quiet, drunken sort of way. As soon as dinner was over, they discreetly went down to their cabin and left us alone. But I doubt that they managed to fall asleep ...

We were sailing in the seas of the Adriatic and it was past midnight; the moon was setting on our left. It was evident that we were on the open sea, as the waves turned from a soft lullabye to an annoying rock. The soft breeze of a few hours ago was becoming stronger and white clouds were circling the moon.

"The weather's going to worsen when we get further out", I said to Jill and waited for her reaction. My experience told me that it wasn't simply going to get worse: it was going to get really bad.

"The sea doesn't bother me", she answered, "but it scares me".

She came and hugged me tightly. I got up and led her into the wheel room. It was already too cool for comfort on deck and the sailors, having seen the same thing I had, were already tidying up the chairs and tables outside.

We sat on the leather sofa behind the wheel, huddled close together in the semi-darkness.

The captain was standing next to the helmsman and looked alternately from the compass to the radar.

"Can you see a storm coming?" I asked him.

He turned to me in surprise, wondering perhaps how I had realized it.

"Not on our route", he answered softly. "There's one much further west, probably near Malta.

I didn't answer, but knew that if the center of the storm was near Malta, it wouldn't be easy going for us, either.

Jill seemed frightened by what we were saying and, more so, by the sight of the raging, dark sea. The captain was trying to gain time by going as quickly northward as possible, but he couldn't go on for long. The sea was getting rougher by the second, with enormous waves rocking the vessel to and fro. Soon he was tacking more softly, saving both the vessel and its passengers from aimless wear and tear. He closed the side door when waves started getting into the wheel room. Then he said something to the helmsman and took the helm with a sure hand. He looked reliable at sea: fiftyish, gray-haired, short but strong, with eyes that pierced the darkness.

Each passing minute brought rougher seas against the boat. The sight was wild, but not dangerous for a vessel of this size. Stars were no longer in sight; a hazy blackness filled the sky. I don't know how far westward the captain had located the storm, but it didn't seem too far from us now.

I got up carefully, holding on to the doorknob, to take a look at the sea. It was obvious that the weather wasn't kidding. Large black masses were hitting the bow, ready to swallow us all. As the boat dipped into them, the wind grabbed parts of the solid mass of water and brought them with force onto the windows of the wheel room. We remained there for ten or twenty seconds before coming up again, seconds that seemed an eternity each time.

The wind was rising and blowing roughly against the sails, which were trying in vain to stay in place against the towering masts of the boat.

There was no doubt that we were very close to the heart of the storm. In spite of the captain's abilities, I couldn't help thinking that he could have avoided it, considering that he had an excellent radar and radio system at his disposal. Moreover, the weather reports must have announced the storm and we could easily have spent the night in the Peloponesse. There was no excuse for getting into this.

The fact was, however, that we were in it for good and the problem now was how to get out safely. The weather, instead of calming down, was still getting wilder and wilder. There were times when it felt like the boat was going to be torn down the middle by the angry waves.

Jill had dug her nails into my arm and was white as a ghost. "There's nothing to be afraid of," I tried to comfort her. "This boat can take twice as rough seeas."

There was no point in telling her that, in fact, it was doubtful if the vessel would survive.

It was just then that we hit on something I had never experienced before: enormous, repeated waves attacked the ship and literally buried us. Previously the waves were hitting only from the left bow; now they were coming from the stern, too, giving us forceful whippings forward against seas that seemed like mountains.

120

It wasn't pleasant by any means. The boat was rocking dangerously and was·obviously in a deep state of suffering. The mast were often almost parallel to the sea, only to come in line with the sky again in terrifying screeches. None of us knew how long it would last and all I could do was just sit and wait for the inevitable splitting in two of the boat.

We were right in the center of the storm. Obviously the captain hadn't estimated well when he spoke of Malta - it could have been near Malta when he saw it, but at the rate of forty or fifty miles an hour northward, it was natural that it would reach us.

Our only hope was that the vessel would last until it was over. I knew that even when it had passed us, the water would be in turmoil for several hours, but it would be peace compared to what we were living through now.

It must have been about two in the morning. There wasn't a light around anywhere. It was pure hell, and we couldn't see a thing. Hell's rage was continuing and the repeated attacks of the waves were a non-stop agony. We had no way of knowing which would be the last.

At some point Jill went into hysterics, justifiably so. Screaming so I could hear, she asked where the lifebelts were.

I turned to her in an attempted smile:

"You must be kidding! What can we do with them?"

I had hardly finished the phrase when the boat jerked towards the right with tremendous force and threw me down. At the same time a loud crash indicated that all the kitchen ware had fallen out of the cupboards and drawers and were crashing against the floor and walls.

The panic that followed was inevitable. Jill was screaming hysterically while I tried to grab onto

121

something and pull myself up. When I managed to do so I grabbed her and held her tightly in my arms, trying to soothe her. She was trembling like a leaf and muttering incoherent sounds.

It seemed like centuries that we stayed that way. The only comfort was that although the weather wasn't any calmer, it wasn't getting worse, either.

Jill was still trembling in my arms but she was at least silent now. It's funny and insane, but it's a fact that no matter how bad a situation is, you get used to it after a while. That's just what had happened to Jill now: she had gotten used to living in hell.

After a while I saw a faint light in the horizon. Daylight was breaking. I lay Jill on the sofa and covered her with a blanket.

I got up again and went near the captain. With the dim light he could easily save the boat from the wild jerks. He turned to look at me with eyes that were bloodshot from sleeplessness and agony.

"It's over", he sighed and sounded as if a knife in his back had been pulled out.

Visibility was getting clearer by the minute. It's amazing how quickly daylight comes on the open seas. In the distance, land could be seen. It must have been the lower cape of Sicily.

"It's over!", I muttered to myself in relief.

We were out of the storm now. Land was beginning to protect us and the sea was finally growing calmer. I turned to look at Jill who was sleeping peacefully. Fatigue had overcome her fear. The helmsman took the wheel again.

The captain and I went down for a cup of coffee, but the sight in the living room was one of total destruction. Nothing was in place: lamps, vases, chairs and tables were in pieces on the floor, rolling with a painting that had come off the wall.

Coffee was brought to us and the captain took his back to the wheelroom. I lay down in a sofa and sleepily drank my coffee. In a few minutes the captain came back down and his bloodshot eyes were in terror.

"I spoke with the coast guard in Syracuse", he said. "At two this morning we passed through the center of the storm with nine beauforts."

"It's impossible", I muttered in disbelief.

What else could I have said? That he had almost drowned us when we could well have spent the night ashore.

I finished my coffee and went back up. Jill was in a deep sleep. I didn't dare move her but just covered her well. Then I went to my cabin and lay down, fully dressed, in my berth. Just before falling asleep, Alexandra came to mind. It must have been her curse, I thought to myself, and dozed off.

CHAPTER 19

After the storm came peace, just as the saying goes.

The next day I woke up at about two in the afternoon, rested and famished. I hurriedly wore my jeans - the only clothing I had - and went up on deck.

Everyone was already sitting around the breakfast table, happy and laughing. They were hungrily eating lunch and drinking cocktails to revive their upset stomachs.

The sea was like a peaceful lake, without a hint of the previous night's turbulence. A beautiful, hot sun warmed us and shined over the mountains of the western coast of Italy. We had passed the straits of Sicily and were sailing parallel to the lovely coast. The captain, still scared after the night's adventures, stayed close to the coastline and so we could see clearly the houses dotting the beach. Soon we would be passing the strait between Capri and Amalfi.

I was welcomed with laughter and jokes. How quickly we get over our fear, I thought, and how shallow people can sometimes be! They seemed to have forgotten the agony of approaching death; now that it was no longer in danger, life was once more theirs to enjoy.

The sea's wrath had hardly touched on them. And why should it? Everything good in life was theirs, life itself belonged to them. Nature sometimes frightened them, but they always came out on top - just like last night: the boat was big and strong and able to survive. That's why it was worth it's money.

We sat around the table, repeating the same stale jokes, talking about their pseudo-problems. I felt like an usher in a theater playing "The Great Gatsby" or "High Society", forced to watch the same performance dozens of times.

I wanted to shout, to open their eyes to the fact that there were other scenarios besides "The Great Gatsby". Instead I ate and drank with them and attempted to lift my spirits. In such cases you either join them or commit suicide.

We were between Capri and Amalfi. The beauty of the scene escaped them; they were more interested in which island has the best night life. At my insistence, we avoided all the spots they had been trying to choose among and we anchored for the night at a small fishing village located between the big names. There was a fantastic little fish tavern where we decided to have dinner. The other customers were a few local fishermen.

I asked the captain and the first mechanic to join us - something which apparently had never happened before. Jill, being a bit of a rebel, enjoyed it. Perhaps she had inherited this trait from her father, when he boot-legged during the prohibition. The other couple, however, didn't seem at all amused - but I couldn't have cared less.

I was joyous to be at this little harbor, away from the cosmopolitan masses vacationing at the various watering spots along the coast. Perhaps, in my subconscious, the place reminded me of faraway Mykonos and the even further away Alexandra ...

We must have eaten half a boatfull of fish and had endless carafes of wine. The fishermen at the next table joined us after a while, and when the discussion focused around last night's storm, they went pale on hearing that we had been right in the middle of it. The storm had evidently caused havoc all over the area and had destroyed several fishing boats in the harbor. I felt at home among the fishermen and their talks of the sea, the sea seems to unit all races and nationalities.

It was past midnight when we decided to return to the boat. Without any need of invitations or explanations, I went straight to Jill's cabin. It was time to pay my fare, but it didn't seem at all a burden.

Jill was unquestionably a beautiful and desirable girl, but with the storm, the other couple always somewhere near, the short time we'd known each other - let alone my infatuation with Alexandra - we hadn't yet really gotten together.

Tonight, however, everything was perfect. Jill had been sweetly leaning on my shoulder throughout the evening at the taverna and listening with interest to my conversation with the fishermen. Perhaps she saw in me a new captain for her boat, a sea version of the prince riding his white horse in fairytales. So when we returned to the yacht, I didn't need an invitation. I just took her by the hand and led her to her cabin.

The cabin, of course, was totally different from the rest. It was rather like a double room in a luxurious hotel. Whether or not she saw me as prince charming of the fairytale, I certainly felt like one. I stretched out on the enormous bed with the silky white bedspread wearing my dirty, faded jeans. I wasn't wearing shoes and my feet had all the signs of going barefoot for three months on Mykonos.

But Jill, being a bit of a hippy like most Americans, wasn't at all perturbed. She just looked at me and burst out laughing. I enjoyed her attitude, which was free of the ridiculous erotic glances of any European woman you take to bed.

She simply took off her shirt and, still wearing her jeans, jumped on the bed and landed next to me.

Jill was a very sweet girl, full of joy and laughter - the epitome of fleeting happiness. She enjoyed all the good things life had in such abundance offered her and didn't ask for more. She was free of complexes and surely it had never crossed her mind that men approached her because of the wealth and beauty that accompanied her.

We played in bed, much in the way I used to play with my daughter when she was a toddler. But suddenly Jill became a woman, and what a woman! A passionate, fiery Irishwoman capable of bringing out the beast in a man.

She knew what she wanted from a man, but she knew how to give, too. She knew when to be a hotblooded bedmate and when to be a loving, tender friend. Above all, she knew well the category of men to which I belong: strong and irresistable lovers on the outside who deep down yearn for tenderness.

Men of this type never show their feelings. They're afraid of seeming likeable or, worse yet, vulnerable to having their feelings be mistaken for weakness. They subdue their spontaneity for fear that the hard exterior - to which they owe their success with women - might melt away. Often they are aware of their delusion, but the force of habit is so strong that it becomes impossible to react differently.

That's more or less what happened with Jill that night. Many times I felt the impact of her tenderness and tended to lean on her shoulder, at least psychologically. She was an oasis in which I could cool off and relax after the anxiety Alexandra had caused. The feelings, of course, were totally different in each case. For Alexandra, I felt anguish and yearning to a point that caused physical pain; Jill filled my being with peace.

I woke up the next day in a sea of serenity, both actual and spiritual. Sipping my coffee in bed, I looked through the porthole upon an incredibly blue and peaceful sea - and if peace is synonymous with happiness, then I was a truly happy man.

The boat was sailing between Corsica and the end of the Italian coastline. In another day we'd be arriving at St. Tropez. Not that I was in the least bit bored; the sea had always been the first and foremost joy in my life. But in this particular case, it wasn't exactly the kind of life at sea I was used to. It was more like living in a floating palace.

Eleven o'clock sharp each morning - never a minute later - the butler, dressed in sparkling white, appeared with the day's first bottle of champagne.

"Don Perignon 1962", he would announce in a low tone, as if a '61 or '63 vintage would have upset my stomach.

If only he could see me on Tasso's caique in Mykonos, gulping down ouzo straight from the bottle and munching on octapus for breakfast! Everything, of course, has its own charm and one should be able to enjoy both the artificial joys as well as the true happiness that lies in simplicity.

It must have been obvious that I was enjoying everything because Jill, rid of the self-control she displayed in the beginning, treated me like her beloved new playmate.

She was a beautiful girl very much so, that played an enormous role in my life. I couldn't even make friends with an ugly woman.

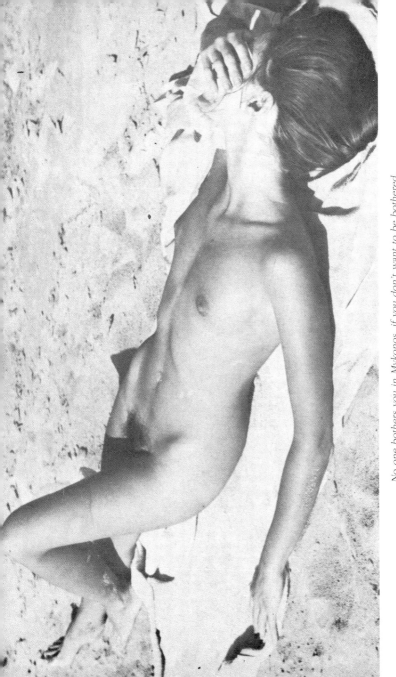

No one bothers you in Mýkonos, if you don't want to be bothered.

The sand and the sun were for Alexandra the great pleasures of a carefree life

Both spent hours lying indifferently under the sun.

Many times Alexandra took poses purposely, to make herself more provocative.

Alexandra always had a perfect joy in her movements.

My worst moments were when one took care of the other.

*There were obvious outbreaks of love between them, that made me feel
hysterically jealous.*

Jill was created by an American God, during a moment of great gaiety and he offered her everything. Everything that a mortal could desire.

It must have been eleven when we went up on deck because the first Don Perignon 1962 had already arrived, followed by John the butler holding an enormous silver tray where, over a layer of ice, two or three dozen delectable oysters were fighting for life. Lemons, tobasco and pepper were standing by to make their death more painful.

We devoured them all and washed them down with two bottles of champagne; a great start for the great day ahead! Jill and I took one of the speedboats so we could go for a swim near the coast of Corsica. When we returned, a cool breeze had appeared and so we set the sails.

By early evening the lights of the Cote d'Azur were visible.

"When are we arriving?" Jill asked the captain.

He came up to us smiling, happy that at last we were close to our destination, and told us we had another 35 miles to go, or about three hours. Just before midnight we were anchoring at St. Tropez.

CHAPTER 20

The entrance to this recently-discovered village in southern France is one of the greatest pleasures to the eye of the beholder.

The village is built in amphitheatrical style, while all the restaurants, clubs and shops are dotted along the harbor. The harbor itself forms a giant crescent where yachts anchor one next to the other.

The pier accommodates about 150 boats, offering a sight which is unique both to those inside the yachts and those sitting along the harbor. Suddenly you enter a different world where attractive boutiques compete with one another and are scattered among bars, restaurants and cafes. After days at sea, the traveller feels that he has finally reached civilization.

For years my dream has been to do the same in Mykonos where, unfortunately, the traveller's first impression is that he's reached nowhere: the pier, located more than half a mile from the island's vibrant center, seems deserted and unattractive to the visitor. Maybe some day people will realize that only the proper scenery can create the proper atmosphere.

As soon as the boat was berthed, we jumped out, thirsty for everything St. Tropez had to offer after so many days at sea. We went into the first bar we saw and started drinking like pirates who finally reached land.

Jill looked delighted to have me next to her; my pleasure was doubled by her laughter and her openess. She was willing to do anything for "us" - she always referred to "us", as in "Where are we heading?" or "Whatever's come over us?"

We didn't stay for long at the bar because it was getting too crowded. The French had finished their dinner and were ready to start drinking again. Instead, we walked along the not-too-crowded harbor, hand in hand, enjoying the evening breeze.

It was a beautiful night with a star-filled sky. The moon, in its last quarter, was rising over the Alpes maritimes, over the highest peak where the village's last houses were perched.

The moon was doing something to me again ... it reminded me of Mykonos, my house, my veranda on the sea - and of course Alexandra. Jill caught on in a flash and firmly pulled me into the Papagallio discotheque.

I was in need of an anesthetic again - Alexandra had to be wiped out of my mind. But meanwhile, what was happening to me? Where was I heading? Where was the one story leading me, and where the other? All these questions tortured me and Jill knew it, so she kept me in a continuous state of erotic stupor. That's why she saw to it that there was always a glass in my hand, be it champagne, scotch or wine.

She was happy when I was dizzy. She was happy, because she didn't feel threatened; she knew that my subconscious was drowsy from the drink.

The headwaiter at Papagallio knew Jill of course and seated us at one of his best tables. The bottle of Don Perignon arrived instantaneously, but, alas, it was younger than those I had become accustomed to: it was a 1965 vintage! Having no other choice, I decided to change my recently acquired habit and drank it. I did another thing that night which wasn't a habit with me. I danced! Jill had me under control again and I was devoted in mind and spirit to her happiness.

We stayed at the disco until the early morning hourse, dancing, chatting and enjoying our first night ashore. Jill didn't want to return to the boat, not even when we left the Papagallio.

"Let's spend the night at the Biblos", she suddenly proposed.

I had stayed at the Biblos once before, a few years back when it had first opened. It's the only good hotel at St. Tropez; all the others are pensions. It's so unusual and bland, however, that it makes you wonder how such a monster could have been built in a such a charming atmosphere.

I remembered the opening night, when Francois Sagan had written in the guest book: "I have no words in which to congratulate you!" It was built by nouveau riche Lebanese businessmen in a supposed Biblical style, with rooms that were like cells, with windows only slightly larger than portholes, with bars on the windows, Arabian-made tiles on the floors and carpets on the walls. My frist impression had been that instead of carpets the decorator should have been hanged on the wall!

It was in this horrid atmosphere that we went to relax - or perhaps to tire - our bodies. They gave us one of those suites whose price makes you stay awake all night. Lying in bed, we looked up to a sky blue silk ceiling.

In typical American fashion, Jill loved the hotel and the pseudo Middle Ages style in which it was built. It was only natural, since people always tend to admire what they've never had, and America never had a Middle Age.

They're a strange people, the Americans. Sometimes you can despise them, but often they're worthy of admiration. Personally, being a totally disorganized individual, I feel deep respect for those who manage to be organized. In this case, Jill had conducted a well-organized Kidnapping that was bound to succeed.

I'm a good loser, as the Americans say; when I lose I admit it with a bitter smile on my lips. Jill had won this round of our little game and, being a good player in life, I accepted it as a fact.

Perhaps she had won me by buying me. In the miserable state of mind she had found me, certainly I felt on sale. The only thing I would never sell was my conscience; and with that in mind I said "yes" without a second thought when Jill invited me to go to Los Angeles with her. It was around noon of our first day at St. Tropez and we were swimming at the Tahiti beach. I took a sip of champagne from the bottle Jill's friend Lot always carried with her. She was like cardiacs who won't make a move without their medicine.

The sun was scorching hot and we dried quickly from both the external heat and the internal heat that all lovers have. There are always two suns for lovers: God's sun on the outside and the devil's sun inside. Jill and I both had the devil's sun inside us. We made a good pair because we were so full of sin and the devil felt at home in our bodies.

CHAPTER 21

The next morning we left for Los Angeles.

The French had given me a permit when we had reached St. Tropez having left Mykonos without a passport and I used it again to board the plane in Nice.

At Los Angeles airport Jill's lawyers were waiting to deposit a few thousand dollars and her invaluable name as a guarantee. Rich countries are for rich people - and there's no denying it.

A black Cadillac was waiting outside. The chauffeur, whose seat was three metres from ours, told Jill how much he had missed the lady while she had been in Europe. All this in the third person and via telephone. Jill thanked him in a condescending tone, without any of the spontaneity that was typical of her. She had become a snob in her country, I realized with horror but didn't comment. Worse signs of her transformation were to follow.

We were on the road to Beverly Hills when she picked up the telephone and said something to the chauffeur. He, in turn, picked up another phone and spoke to someone. In a few minutes two motorcycles appeared, driven by policemen. They went ahead and, driving like madmen through red lights, opened they way for us.

At first I didn't quite understand; it was totally unfathomable. All my life I had avoided hurrying. Why was I supposedly in a hurry now? To go where, to meet whom? I hated having anyone wait for me, I felt that time limits shorten life. I never wore a watch. Why was my life being changed now by these racing policemen?

I didn't say a word, but my patience was wearing thin. Jill was looking at me through the corner of her eye to see my reaction to her brainstorm. When she saw the look on my face she knew I wasn't exactly pleased. Now she wanted to get rid of our escorts but it was hard. We went on silently for another ten minutes and when we got into Sunset Boulevard she told the driver to stop.

The policemen pulled up next to us and smiled at Jill. She discreetly handed them a fifty dollar bill and they disappeared.

We continued towards Jill's house in Beverly Hills, without police escort thankfully. Jill became her pleasant self again, pointing out to me the fantastic houses of Hollywood's past glories - Clark Gable, Gloria Swanson, Errol Flynn. Some were inhabited, others abandoned, all of them with the sad grandeur of a glory forever gone.

We left the boulevard behind us and started the climb up the hills. On either side, magnificent creations of imaginative architecture sprang up from the lush greenery. Each of them different, but blended together in exquisite harmony.

It was like Alice in wonder land: Frank's Sinatra's Mexican ranch; Tina Turner's French manor; Cary Grant's English mension. The owners all famous, wealthy, talented, living in the beauty of harmony and wealth.

We reached Jill's house which, I had to admit, was among the most attractive. It reminded me of the charming old French houses still standing on Victor Hugo Avenue, where the Boulogne forest begins.

My guess was right. It had been built before the war by the king of French humor, Adolfe Manjou, and had been bought by Jill's mother shortly before his death. Manjou had been forced to sell it in order to live his last few years respectably.

We went up to the second floor bedrooms. Jill headed straight for hers while her maid followed with her suitcases. I was led to mine, carrying my only luggage: a sweater I had bought in St. Tropez and wearing the mocassins the captain had loaned me. I had, after all, started out on this crazy sojourn barefoot!

The house's interior was also French and indicative of the taste of its owner, who for years had been considered the best-dressed man in Hollywood.

I stretched out on the bed with great pleasure. The twelve-hour flight had made me feel rusty and an hour's nap revived me. When Jill came to wake me up with a tender hug I felt terrific. She told me it was almost seven and I had to get up to try on the pants she had ordered for me. I needed something to wear that night, she said, and in case alterations were needed they had to be done in time.

If I had had all the pants she bought for me in Mykonos, I would have opened the island's three hundred and seventy-third boutique. Anyhow, I tried one on for size and it fit perfectly. A shirt by Nina Ricci and the captain's mocassins, freshly shined, completed my outfit for the warm Hollywood night.

Feeling fresh and relaxed, I was able to admire Jill's exotic little paradise. We had gone straight to the bedrooms when we arrived so I really hadn't seen much.

We went to the back side of the house which looked out to a garden straight out of a fairytale. A heart-shaped pool was in the middle of this paradise. The living room, reading room and and dining room all faced the garden.

We sat by the pool where, in spite of the trees and the water, the air was warm. Immediately a black dressed in white appeared, pushing a portable bar. Jill was a charming hostess who tried and succeeded in making me almost as happy as herself.

"I'm going to throw a big party for you!" she exclaimed suddenly. I didn't answer right away, but thought that such a party would certainly be an attraction for me, something like visiting the Statue of Liberty or the Empire State Building.

I told her it sounded like a good idea, that I'd like to see the way in which the American aristocracy amused itself.

We went out for a quiet dinner to discuss plans for the party. My first taste of America was a restaurant which Jill asumed would remind me of home. Thankfully, she didn't choose a Greek restaurant complete with bouzouki players - there are plenty in Los Angeles. Instead, we went to a Moroccan place, considered one of the best in Los Angeles. It may have been fashionable, but personally I didn't find it to be one of the best.

We sat on some pillows which I seriously doubt the Moroccans find comfortable and ate, without the aid of silverware, a very common roast beef served by a filthy-looking Arab who stood over our heads.

Just as I had finished the meat and felt as filthy as the waiter looked, he re-appeared carrying an enormous bowl of water to wash our hands in.

Jill's enthusiasm over the restaurant waned when I told her I had lived for five years in Arab countries and had never eaten with my hands. Naturally we were unable to discuss the party, since we divided our time between getting greasy and washing up. When we got home after my first Arabian night in America I rushed into a hot tub and scrubbed myself with passion.

Our other nights were just as exotic: Chinese, Rumanian Hungarian, but never American. I wasn't surprised, because I knew of only one real American restaurant, and that was in London: The Great American Disaster.

Meanwhile invitations for the party were being prepared. Looking at the list, I felt that I would be among old friends. Funny, how there's a whole world of people with whom our lives are connected but whom we've never met. It's common in Los Angeles to run into the aged Fred Astaire at a restaurant and remember your childhood; to have a drink next to the ageless Cary Grant at some watering spot. And if you ask the person at the next table for a light, it could turn out to be Warren Beatty, as it did with me. Not only did he give me a light but, being alone and bored, he started a conversation with me.

I was at the bar of the Beverly Hills hotel waiting for Jill and he was sitting on the next stool waiting for his siter, Shirley MacLaine. His sister came first and when Jill arrived she found the three of us chatting and drinking together.

When the Hollywood crowd realizes that you're not one of them and that you're not American, they tend to find you more interesting than you find them! Human nature is such, that even if you live in paradise it sometimes bores you and you look for something new and different.

CHAPTER 22

The next day Jill woke up rather earlier than usual and woke me up, too.

"Get up", she ordered, "I have a surprise for you today!"

Surprises are not usually my cup of tea and I wasn't sure just how far the humor of others could reach, I persuaded Jill to tell me what was awaiting me.

She had arranged with the president of Universal, she told me over breakfast, to take me on a tour of the studios' inner sanctums. I have to admit that the surprise was not only pleasant, but beyond what I might have hoped for. Since my early youth I had been impressed and attracted by Hollywood's behind-the-scenes.

We set out early and were soon in the famous San Fernando Valley. Anything related to the movies is famous for me, and San Fernando is the valley of the movie industry. Motels, filling stations, super markets and coffee shops were tastefully situated on either side of the road.

An enormous, strange city greeted us at one point.

"Are we arriving?" I asked Jill.

"Not yet", she answered. "This is the Warner Brothers studio which was bought by Universal".

The further we drove, the more it was as if we were leaving a wasteland behind us and entering a giant city without boundaries. We passed by the Warner studio and went on to Universal. More selters and more cities that looked better than real as the California sun shined down on them.

We went on for a few more miles and reached the big gates with a sign saying "Universal studios, keep out".

In spite of the "keep out" sign Jill went on with the confidence of someone driving a fifteen thousand dollar car. She stopped at the inner gate and two policemen jumped up and approached the car. Jill gave them her name which once again worked magic. Their attitude changed at once and the gates opened wide.

We went on to studio 5l, where Ernie Kowalsky, the Mexican who was Universal's newest find in the field of film directing, greeted us. He was the perfect guide to the inner sanctums. The three of us got into an electric car and the tour began under the brilliant sun that shines on California all year round.

In the streets among the various studios a whole new world of people was rushing to and fro. It's one thing I can never really understand about America, this continuous rush of its people. Every nationality on earth must have been represented among the individuals who were hurrying with papers, scenery, scenarios, luggage or a thousand other things in their hands. Occasionally one would stop for a minute to chat with another and then hurry on even more quickly, to gain the minute lost.

Meanwhile, I was staring at the little identical houses lining the street. They all had two windows and a door with a sign on it: Charlton Heston, Telly Savalas, Ray Milland, Jacquelie Bisset, Laureen Bacall, Alfred Hitchcock and a host of other famous and not-so-famous names.

The answer I got when I asked what all these little houses were used for, was that each actor or director has one in order to rest between takes or to stay overnight when there's an early morning shooting.

We passed by the streets with the houses and drove on to another which had a country atmosphere about it. Soon we were in cities full of trees and gardens; the fake ones looked just as real as the real ones. Old American houses in western style brought you into another world. I learned that the street represented a suburb of New Orleans and that the houses had been transported from there.

The scenery lasted for about five hundred meters and, suddenly, we were in Paris! And when I say in Paris, I don't mean in a Parisian decor, but in Paris itself! Real, imposing, but totally deserted.

The car stopped and I got out. What I found most incredible was the detail in every single structure. The street we were on was the one in which Gene Kelly had done "Singing in the Rain."

When I turned to Kowalsky and told him that we were on Rue Delambre, he wondered how I knew it.

"I lived on Rue Delambre 9 when Gene Kelly and the crew came to shoot Singing in the Rain in 1959", I explained.

This strange coincidence made all three of us think of the unusual things that sometimes happen. I examined the details of the houses and just couldn't believe it. It was a street I knew so well, leaving in the morning and returning again for years. The doors were exactly the same, the numbers were right, even the grayish hue of all Parisian houses was there.

We went on silently through other streets; the only sound was that of our footsteps. Only the deserted look and the silence made you aware that it wasn't for real. Everything else was so perfect that it was almost scary:

As we were walking on, a group of dancers suddenly came out of a side street. They gave the setting some movement, some life, but only for a few minutes. They were soon gone into another street led by the director.

From a frighteningly real but deserted Paris we passed a wooden door and found ourselves in a London that was just as real and just as deserted. The details were all there, all the way.

We got back into the little car and drove on to another faraway world, one brimming with life and action. In my movie-trained imagination, it must have been Oklahoma's wild west. Robbers, cowboys and sheriffs were involved in a deathly duel; horses and people fell and got up again; shots were heard all around and the air was full of dust.

As soon as the battle was over we put up our hands and gave ourselves up to the sheriff. The director was a friend of Kowalsky's and he told us all about the secrets of cowboys and Indians over a coffee break.

Right after the borders of Oklahoma, Roman palaces appeared. After walking a while among columns and ruins we reached an area where a historical film was being shot. I saw Jesus Christ reading a newspaper a few feet away from Pontius Pilate having a Coke.

A bit further away we stopped and I saw a fantastically beautiful girl get up to greet Kowalsky. It was Jacqueline Bisset and I almost fainted when we were introduced. I had met many stars, but that wasn't the point. She was so terrific I couldn't get over it; even when we were touring other areas of the studio my mind stayed with her. Jill, sharp as always, realized it and asked if I was tired. Several hours had passed and our tour was almost over.

Soon we were back where we had started and, after hugs and kisses between Jill and Kowalsky and promises that he would come to her party, we left. I felt like Alice leaving Wonderland.

That night we slept at Jill's beach house at Malibu. The waves were beating against the house all night and lulled us to sleep.

CHAPTER 23

Two hundred and fifty invitations had been sent out for the party. It was to be held the following week but by this time I had lost the conticipation brought by new experiences in life.

Day by day the things that had seemed spectacular at first were beginning to feel commonplace and, along with them, Jill was also losing her original charm. She tried in every way to please me and seemed almost in love; but instead of making me happier the situation tended to get on my nerves.

I was beginning to get bored and that was at the heart of the problem. Moreover, I didn't find Jill attractive anymore - especially when she was drunk. There was no logic to it, I know, since I had met her drunk and had followed her halfway around the world drunk. But now it got on my nerves and sometimes it even disgusted me.

Things weren't going well - that was a fact. The explosion hadn't come yet, but it was on the way. I realized that I had to make a decision instead of waiting for the explosion. The problem, however, was that Alexandra had started appearing in my thoughts and my dreams again; I tried to chase her away by persuading myself that it was great where I was, that I had found love, tenderness and care - just the kind of serenity needed for my mixed-up emotions.

Time to time all the money made Jill take miens and poses of an empress.

Sitting next to the cape, where she anchored the cutter, she alone enjoyed the open sea.

For everyone besides me who was going through a sentimental trial with Alexandra, Jill was a dream like creation.

Even naked Jill always found something to fix herself. An American conquetry form.

Lying on the beach, Jill looked like a lovely living statue.

There's no rarer phenomenon than to see Mykonos with such a "stain"

Even the beach of Venice deadened after the first rains.

The taxis stopped in the square of Mado. Unusual phenomenon (winter photograph).

Unfortunately my attempts brought the opposite results. Instead of calming down, I was filled with anxiety and longing for my house, for Mykonos, for my friends. Most of all I longed for Alexandra.

I had started feeling totally foreign to all the beautiful things around me and, when the day of the party finally arrived, my mood was negative. There was no enthusiasm for all the famous and beautiful people I would be meeting that night.

Jill had noticed the change that had come over me and tried occasionally to win me back; other times she would stop caring and probably thought to herself, if he doesn't like it, he can just get up and leave. In either case she drank too much.

Two days ago food and liquor for the party had started arriving. We could have opened a luxury super market with the orders that were coming in: cases of champagne, giant cans of caviar and smoked salmon, two enormous refrigerator cases of live oysters flown in from Mexico, cases of genuine Russian vodka, cheese from France and more and more that could have supplied a large hotel for a month. I would go down to the kitchens and stare for hours at the latest arrivals.

The night of the party, everything was in order at seven o'oclock. The guests started arriving in groups of seven or eight. I was sitting at the bar by the pool and watching them come in. Jill was coming and going, greeting them at the entrance and bringing them into the garden area. Like rats smelling for cheese, they would throw uneasy glances around in search of the liquor. Jill knew them well and had set up four bars around the garden, in addition to the one where I was sitting.

The first groups of arrivals were not well known. The

145

stars would come later, with the usual delay of famous and secure people. The garden was filling up and soon the big names started showing.

The first group was headed by Dean Martin and there was definitely a different aura about the people who were with him. The women were something else - tall, exotic-looking, dressed to kill. The earlier arrivals swarmed around them, but soon their attention was caught by the next group: "The Great Gatsby" was being shot at the time and the entrance of Robert Redford with Mia Farrow and their co-stars was the evening's main attraction. Meanwhile it had gotten so crowded that it was difficult to distinguish who was who.

I realized that my seat at the bar was the best observation point and I wouldn't part with it for anything. Most of the guests would pass by, stare at me, mutter a hello and go off wondering who I was. My face reminded them of nothing and they assumed I was some great European personality. I enjoyed the mystery that had surrounded me and, since Jill had either lost me or forgotten me, I was able to retain it. If, after all, she had told them that she had picked me up literally barefoot in a bar in Mykonos they would have been greatly disappointed!

My little game didn't last for long unfortunately. Smiling, swaying and drunk, Jill was heading straight for my corner with shouts of "Darling, where have you been? I want to introduce you around!"

Introduce me to who, I wondered. By this time the drink and the dope had worked their magic and the guests were beginning to forget each other. The last thing on earth they wanted was to make new acquaintances.

She was next to me now, emptying her glass of

champagne down my throat. After several vodkas, it worked wonders in lifting my spirits. Jill took me by the hand and started parading me around the garden. Our first stop - with an intermediate one to fill up on champagne - was to meet a group of five with unknwon to me faces. I didn't quite catch their names but it made no difference. What I did notice was the women's dresses. Women in Los Angeles are not generally known for their modest attire, but tonight they had outdone themselves.

Two of the three women in the group wore gowns with necklines to the navel, while the third had completely thrown out the top and wore instead a little shawl around her neck; her breasts were playing hide'n seek under its silk fringes. One of the three turned around to greet someone and I noticed in surprise that the same style adorned their back sides: three-quarters of her behind was on display: The third revelation in Hollywood fashion came when one of them sat down and crossed her legs: the dress was slit at the sides up to her waist. As she sat down, I imagine I, the underdeveloped Greek, was the only one who assumed she was wearing panties. Of course I was wrong, and soon realized that Jill, too, was pantyless!

While I was making discoveries about local fashion trends, Jill was telling her friends that I was Greek - the genuine article, not one from Chicago, that she had met me on a Greek island, and so on. The same scenario was repeated with several other groups of Jill's friends. I have to admit that the women were all stunning in appearance and the men, too, were attractive - even though at least half of them were obviously homosexual. They were all drunk and seemed to be having fun.

It wasn't only the drink that made them that way: it

was also the silver cigarette boxes that Jill passed around from time to time. In order to please her friends, she had loaded them with marijuana and one was enough to send you to seventh heaven.

The fact was, however, that they were still on earth. The only flying objects were pieces of cake and ice cream that they were throwing at each other, one of the great American passtimes. The ones who had been attacked tried to clean off the mess with champagne but it was futile. It was Jill who finally found the solution: she was the first to dive into the pool pulling two men with her, one on each side.

The others didn't need long to catch on. In a few minutes the pool was filled with men and women, some dressed and some rid of their clothing. Some of the guests managed to get away in time, while the waiters - apparently used to such antics discreetly withdrew. And so some forty people - male female and homosexuals - remained in the pool. They shouted, laughed, pulled each other around and undressed one another.

Jill was the first to get out with two others girls. They were all nude, of course, and ran into the house to get towels. The others followed in the same direction and soon the party had been transferred to the second floor with the eight bedrooms and the eight bathrooms.

A strange silence filled the garden, much like the silence that follows a storm. The lights were turned off by a servant and only the lights from the second floor windows allowed me to look at the miserable view of the garden. Tables and chairs were overturned; the pool looked like a filthy swamp with pieces of chocolate, swirls of whipped cream and shreds of expensive gowns floating on its surface.

148

I don't remember how long I stood there looking at the mess before deciding to see what the others were doing.

CHAPTER 24

The laughter and the screams were heard more and more clearly as I went up the stairs. It was easy to guess the condition in which the guests were in.

When I reached the top I looked into a bathroom whose door was open and saw the same picture of calamity that prevailed in the garden - only here there was a nude woman sitting on the bathtub with her head immersed in water. I thought perhaps she wasn't feeling well and went in to offer help. I was mistaken. She was, in fact, helping the man in the tub feel better. I left them and closed the door behind me, almost stumbling on a man who was lying on the sofa in the hallway with his arms and legs dangling.

I went on to my room and thought I'd make a stop to see how Jill was doing. The door to my room was open and I imagined that perhaps she was waiting for me inside. Another mistake: all over my bed various forms of the sexual act were taking place.

Two girls were lying on the bed, and neither of them was Jill. One of them was lying back side up with a man behind her who was moaning. The other one had a man's head between her legs which she was pulling towards her with passion. He was kneeling by the bed and, much as the girl tried, she couldn't pull him any closer - another man was screwing him from behind.

As soon as the girl saw me she left the man's head and asked me to join her:

"Hey, you! Come here!"

Someone else had entered the room after me and he went towards her. Without any care about which one of us it was, she grabbed him and they started making love.

I left the room with a strange feeling: it was neither a sexual turn-on nor disgust. The girl was so beautiful, that I rather felt sorry.

Heading for Jill's room I stumbled on the man on the sofa again. This time a woman was lying over him and she was trying to make him recover. Laughing she turned to me: "I think he's dead!" she announced.

She went on laughing hysterically and gave him a slap which must have knocked half his teeth out. He came to, groaned and pulled her on top of him.

I went on to find Jill. The room's door was closed but just as I got there it opened and a naked man came out.

"Go on in", he said. "There's a vacancy!"

I entered, thinking I was prepared for the scene I was to witness. I imagined something similar to what was going on in my room, but this time I was really shocked. A heavy smell of marijuana filled the room. The two lights by Jill's bed were on and I could clearly see that it was her lying in it.

She was nude, of course, with her head resting on another girl. A man was kneeling over her chest with her body between his legs. He was holding her head with both hands and had shoved his entire penis into her mouth.

Sitting further down was a queer who was laughing hysterically and holding Jill's legs open for a fat, sweaty man who was trying to screw her.

There was even more perversion going on in that room: the man who was holding Jill's head between his hands was being whipped from behind by another man. He was beginning to bleed, and the sight of blood made the other man whip him even more savagely. I thought for a minute that the bleeding man must have no control of himself and that he might choke Jill; but then I realized that she must be used to this kind of play and knew how to protect herself.

She managed to free her head for a minute and let out a long scream which sounded familiar - it was the sound of Jill's orgasm. Then her head fell to the side, but the man kneeling over her grabbed it again and once more shoved his penis down her throat.

Jill had stopped reacting. She opened her eyes for a minute and looked at me with a vacant stare; I doubted she recognized me. She seemed to be choking and her eyes were terribly blood-shot. Choked screams were coming from her throat but nothing could stop the bleeding maniac on top of her who was coming in her mouth. He suddenly let out a heavy groan and then fell back exhausted. The man who had been whipping him turned the bloody body around and started fucking him like a dog.

Jill, by this time, had vomited and was lying in the pool of champagne, expensive wines, caviar and the sperms of at least one man. The fat man was now stretched out on top of her and trying desperately to come. The queer had left them and was rolling on the floor with the bloody pair.

I was ready to leave when another man came into the room. He looked around and headed straight for Jill. He pulled the fat man from her and lifted her from the filthy bed to a fur rug on the floor. Kneeling over her, he gave her soft and then harder and harder slaps until she came to. She stared at him for a minute and then with a violent movement she pulled him to her and they started making love.

Like a robot I went to my room, remembering that there was some money in my drawer. I took it and went down the stairs and out the door.

I took a deep breath of fresh air when I got out and started walking down Beverly Hills. Everything was so quiet and dark around me! Not a soul was on the street, and the first rays of light were rising from behind the hills.

I reached Sunset Boulevard and stood on a street corner smoking a cigarette and thinking over the night's experiences. I hadn't really been bothered by all I had seen, but a kind of Mediterranean sense of dignity made me feel ashamed. I was wondering how these people, after all they had done to and with each other, would meet the next day in a chic restaurant or bar or in the office and say hello as if nothing had happened!

A patrol car stopped in front of me and a tall black policeman came out.

"What are you doing here?" he wanted to know.

"I'm waiting for a taxi", I answered absent-mindedly, "to take me to the airport so I can go back to Mykonos".

He didn't seem to understand what I was talking about and he certainly wouldn't imagine that the heaven on earth called Mykonos existed.

"You'll probably end up at the morgue", he answered, "if you stay here much longer!"

You can't even enjoy the sunrise alone in America! There's always the danger that someone will stab you for your money!

He took me by the hand and led me into the car. We finally reached a point where there were lights and taxis.

"Here's your taxi", he said and opened the door for me.

He told the driver to take me to the airport and asked me if I had money. I showed him the wad of bills I had taken from my drawer and he in turn showed it to the driver. He also wrote down the driver's name and license number. It was like saying, if you kill him for the money, we know who you are!

I got into the cab and instantly fell asleep. The driver awakened me when we reached the airport.

CHAPTER 25

When you look down on America from an airplane it's hard to imagine all the tragic and great things that happen below.

The sun was shining over Los Angeles' and had drenched it in sparkle and beauty; the sun's rays were shimmering on the skyscrapers of glass and nickel as we passed over them.

I had chosen a seat in the back of the jumbo and, since the aircraft was half-empty, I made myself a cozy bed over five seats. I spent ten of the flight's twelve hours sleeping peacefully and without nightmares.

When we landed in London the very atmosphere lifted my spirits. I felt as if I had landed in Paradise, and Paradise was my home. Smiling to myself I boarded the plane for Athens two hours later. I felt back home as soon as I was in the aircraft; "The pilot wishes you a pleasant trip. In three hours and ten minutes we will be landing in Athens."

It all seemed too good to be true; I felt as if I was waking up from a nightmare, or coming back from the jungle. I was, in fact, returning from the wildest jungle on earth!

Even though I was travelling economy class a stewardess who knew me offered me a glass of champagne. It was impolite to turn it down, but champagne was the last drink on earth I wanted.

"You're going to spoil me", I kidded.

"It's too late for that", she smiled back. "You've been spoiled all your life!"

And how right she was! I did the craziest things in life, and got away with it! A month ago I set out with a perverted nut, not even knowing where we were headed for. But why shouldn't I? Doesn't every one of us take advantage of the weaknesses of others when he can? If I hadn't gone, I would have been more honest towards myself and a more "serious" person - but for me there are far too many serious people in this world already!

The landing in Athens was announced; I had never felt such joy and relief on returning to Greece. Although it was late autumn, winter seemed far away. A pleasant, warm sunshine spread over the Saronic Gulf.

I knew why I felt so good, but I didn't dare admit it even to myself: I was near ... near a girl who for the past month and a half had caused me such intense pain and pleasure.

Feeling like a schoolboy calling a girl on a first date, I dialed her number in Athens. There was no answer.

Then I started to call Marilena but the thought of her turned me off; I didn't really care how she was doing and I was in no mood to listen to her sarcastic remarks. I put the receiver down again, annoyed at myself for hating her. A mature person shouldn't have such weaknesses and hate, after all, its a weakness.

Having no luggage to burden me, I walked over to the bar and ordered a beer to clear up my thoughts. The simplest thing to do was to go home and make my calls from there - I realized that but something kept me at the airport. Suddenly I decided to try the house in Mykonos;

my friend Billy should be there at this time and he could tell me the news.

I dialed the number and after three rings a voice that shocked me picked it up and repeated "hello" several times before I was able to answer.

Alexandra was still in Mykonos and answering the telephone in my house! I couldn't believe it!

As soon as she heard my voice she started shriekling into the phone:

"It's you! Where on earth are you?"

"Yes, it's me", I mumbled "What's going on?"

"What do you mean, what's going on? Where are you?"

I had gotten over my initial surprise and was able to answer more calmly:

"Instead of screaming, why don't you tell me what's the matter? I'm in Athens."

"And where have you been all this time?" She went on in the same tone.

"I was in America, Alexandra, and please stop screaming!"

"Congratulations! Did you leave in that yacht?"

"Yes", I answered drily.

"Someone had told me they saw you and I didn't believe it!"

My disappearance had made miracles, I began to think!

"How soon can you get here?" Alexandra asked.

"I'm at the airport, and if there's a five o'clock flight I'll be on it."

"Yes, there's a flight. Get on it and come quickly! she said, still yelling.

"O.K., I'm coming", I answered calmly. "Wait for me at home."

"No!", she shouted as if I had said something terrible,

"I'll meet you at the airport!"

I agreed and hung up. I was trembling with joy, not only because I had found her, but also because she sounded anxious to see me! After the disheartening adventure in America, I was beginning to feel once more like a human being, one that was in love with a girl that returned his feelings.

I ran to the counter and purchased a ticket for Mykonos. The plane was taking off in a half hour. Then I went back to the bar but this time I didn't order beer. What could beer do for me, feeling the way I did? Liquid gunpowder would have been more like it!

I was an emotional wreck. I was thrilled, I was mixed up, I was anxious, but most of all I was scared to death of the little tin can resembling an airplane that would be taking me Mykonos. Furthermore, it was a windy day - and when it's windy in Athens, in Mykonos there's a hurricane!

By the second scotch my anxiety had been greatly reduced, and by the fourth I was boarding the tin car, filled with joy that I would soon be seeing the woman I loved!

The ups and downs of the aircraft brought back my fears again, by the time we were about to land I was a bit wary. I hadn't after all, thought about what Alexandra was doing in Mykonos at this time of year. And then the terrible question had to be answered: Was Marilena on the island too? I tried to push the thought away. If she really was there, then why did Alexandra sound so eager to see me?

A terrifying jolt of the airplane brought me back to my senses. What good was love and happiness if it crashed? A look out the window helped to calm me? we were circling

158

over Psarrou beach and preparing to land.

God, what a beautiful place the island was! It was cloudy, and yet everything was snow-white, sparkling, so deserted and romantic!

If what I felt was happiness, then I wanted nothing else in life. When the sea darkens and the houses look whiter under the clouds, no plane could possible crash! You had to live to enjoy it!

And, strangely enough, it looked as if I could survive. The plane was on the runway and I could see Alexandra waiting outside. I was the first to jump off the plane and started running towards her. Halfway there, I realized with a start that there seemed to be no enthusiasm on her part. She was standing there motionless, with a harsh, frozen smile on her lips. Suddenly her words on the phone came to mind: "Come quickly! No, don't come home, I'll meet you at the sirport." If the words had been uttered with the same look she had on her face now, my joy had been in vain.

In seconds I had realized my mistake, but was still unable to give myself an explanation for her attitude.

Trying not to give away my thoughts, I swept her into my arms and kissed her. It was like kissing a lifeless doll at first, but soon she broke down. She pulled me closer and started weeping uncrontrollably, as if she needed someone to lean on.

She took me by the hand and walked towards Nicolas' taxi, which was waiting for us.

As soon as we got in, Nicolas turned and asked me in a simple, straightforward manner:

"Where the hell have you been all this time?"

"In America", I answered. "Now shut up and drive!"

We drove on in silence. Three times I started to ask if

Marilena was there, but I didn't dare. Patience, I told myself. I'll soon find out.

When we reached the harbor we got off and Alexandra led me to a coffee house. I sat down and took a deep breath. The incredible experiences of the past fortyeight hours had broken me down physically and mentally; all I wanted was to get some sleep. At this point, I didn't even care if Marilena was still there. Not that I had stopped worrying over my future with Alexandra, but I felt like someone who has been cross-examined for two days and finally breaks down and admits he is guilty - anything, to get some rest.

"Alexandra, let's finish our coffee and go home, sweetheart. I have to get some sleep."

She didn't show any reaction. She took a sip of coffee and started to say something. Just then, I felt a friendly tap on my shoulder and turned around. It was Thanassis, the doctor.

"Hi, there!" I welcomed him.

He pulled up a chair and sat with us.

"Surely you must have heard the news", he said.

The look on my face indicated that I didn't know what he was talking about.

"I'm talking about the girl", he explained.

"What girl?" I asked anxiously, my eyes opened wide in fear. I turned to Alexandra. She had a decisive look on her face, as if she was finally ready to make an important announcement.

A thousand terrible things passed through my mind in a matter of seconds. I was afraid that something unspeakably bad had happened to Alexandra, even if she was sitting next to me looking perfectly healthy.

I grabbed her shoulders and asked in agony:

Billy's bar will soon be closed for ever. A rich man bought it to shelter museum objects. What sort of charity is this leaving a poor man on the street?

They don't whitewash anymore. The rains washed away the lime.

The streets were "deserted" when winter came in.

The chairs on the beaches empty with the first rain falls.

A rainy cloudy morning. The beach smelt of rain.

Few were the passer-by's on the beach the first winter rains had started.

No tragic ending is worse than the endless waiting. "The last boat arrived, but Alexandra wasn't inside ...."

Manto a beautiful specimen of Myconean bravery is struck by the north winds that wildly traverse the island, summer and winter. Her marble glare gazes into the most azure sea on earth.

"Alexandra, tell me what's wrong with you!"

Thanassis was looking on with a sorry look on his face. After what seemed an eternity, Alexandra finally spoke:

"It's Marilena, dear! It's Marilena", she managed to say and started sobbing again.

I'm ashamed to admit it, but I was relieved to know that it wasn't Alexandra that Thanassis had refereed to.

I turned to Thanassis, hoping he could enlighten me. But she wiped her eyes and started talking:

"Remember when she had left to Athens for two days?"

How could I ever forget those two days, I thought but didn't say anything. She went on:

"She had gone to pick up some X-rays from the doctor. They had been taken before she came here with you. She came, suspecting that something was wrong. That's why she tried to enjoy herself as much as possible, fearing that it may well be her last vacation. But even in that she was unlucky: she chose you.

"What on earth are you talking about?" I interrupted her, annoyed that I didn't understand any of what she was telling me. "Stop the rhetoric and tell me what's wrong. What do you mean, last vacation? What the matter with Marilena? Or is she already dead?"

"Stratis, she's going to die. And soon! It's a matter of days, because her body is filled with cancer. That's what I've been trying to tell you. So stop shouting and listen!"

I turned to Thanassis, hoping it was all a bad dream.

"That's the way it is, Stratis. I saw the X-rays she brought from Athens. She has no hope. You won't recognize her when you see her."

It was more than I could take. Now, to top off everything, I felt guilty, tragically guilty. How could I have ever imagined such things when I set out with her two months before?

"And why don't we take her to the hospital?" was all I could say. "She wants to stay here. Thanassis is caring for her", Alexandra answered between sobs.

"And isn't there any hope at all?" I asked Thanassis.

His nod meant, absolitely none.

I was so surprised and felt such grief that I just couldn't believe it. Everything had happened so quickly, like a flash. Now I had to face the worst experience of all.

I had to go see Marilena at the house. A Marilena who would be unrecognizable, ready to depart for another world, a world that might be cold and lonely, a world without light. Poor Marilena, who had adored the bright sun of Mykonos, the warm beaches, the beautiful people around her!

They had both stopped talking. I had stopped asking questions. Death and grief had taken over.

"Let's go", I said and got up. I went ahead, Thanassis and Alexandra behind. No one spoke. It was like a procession for a funeral that was about to happen.

I stopped at the glistening white church near the house, the one that Marilena had so admired. I couldn't go on ... the house was only a few steps away.

CHAPTER 26

Much as I tried, my footsteps wouldn't take me any further. I went around the church and stood on its porch from where I gazed on the most beautiful sea on earth.

The reflection of the clouds - that special bright grey - gave the sea under the cliff a shiny green color which allowed the eye to see all the way down to its sparkling depths. Looking down, the words of a girl I had once loved came to mind: "Stratis, when you die I shall bury you in the sea ..."

Fatigue and grief brought back far-away remembrances and visions. With a sure step, I turned around and headed for the house. The others had already gone in.

There was a sharp bite on my soul as I entered. The door was open and I went into the dimly lit living room. A pungent, medicinal smell was in the air.

I went straight to my room and sat on the bed, not knowing what else to do. Alexandra heard me and came in. She sat next to me and kissed me on the cheek, a kiss containing a little love and much sadness. She could see what I was going through and tried to help. She, perhaps, was used to the ghost of death wandering around us.

"Come, we'll go see her", she said and took me by the hand.

I followed her blindly and went into the room ... but no, it couldn't be true. Surely the vision lying on the bed was not a human being, not the girl I had left, full of life, a month ago.

All that was left of the cute, pixie-like face were two huge, dull, protruding black eyes which took up most of the face. The rest seemed to have been glued to the bones, which jutted out where the cheekbones used to be, covered by a waxen, yellow skin.

There was no blood in her body, and if there was, it must have been yellow, too. She was breathing heavily and her eyes were glued to the ceiling.

I stood there staring at her, speechless.

Alexandra was stroking her face and Marilena turned to look at her with a frozen, expressionless gaze. Thanassis was holding her wrist - or what was left of it - and taking her pulse rate.

"Marilena, it's Stratis! He's come back, he's with us now!"

With the mention of my name, her face jerked with a little spasm and the yellow skin stretched even more over the bones. Slowly she turned her eyes toward me and she tried to smile. Her lips moved with a dry sound, dry and chapped as they were. I leaned over to hear if she was trying to say something: it sounded like "Hi!" and it was filled with pain.

Then she turned her head, closed her eyes and started breathing even more heavily. For days she didn't utter another word; I'm still not sure whether it was "Hi" or "Bye" she had whispered to me on her deathbed.

I walked out of the room as if in a nightmare. Thanassis left, saying he would drop by the next day. What was the use? What did the poor thing get out of living in that condition?

Alexandra went into the kitchen to make some soup

for her. Providing, of course, she would manage to get some spoonful into her. The passion with which she tried to keep Marilena alive was one of those things that nature dictates, even though we never really know why.

To the contrary, I was a much more practical person. Just as I believe in good living, I also believe in mercy killing. God and the church have ordered doctors not to do it. Where is the wisdom in it? Why must man suffer in his attempt to die? The quicker one's death, the better. At least you depart with pleasant memories of life!

That night Alexandra and I went out, There was no point in staying home; for hours Marilena would fall into comas without end.

Alexandra was living intensely through all of Marilena's agony, but still I was unable to figure out just what she felt for her. Whatever they may have been, pain and sorrow were clearly outlined on her face.

She was well justified as a woman she was more vulnerable to the pain of others. I tried in every way to make her realize the fact that none of us would stay in this world forever. To my own surprise, I discovered once more, in the midst of the tragic atmosphere we were living in, how hopelessly jealous of her I was. Even if her feelings for Marilena were only pain and sorrow, still I was jealous.

Within a few hours of my arrival the old anxiety for Alexandra was back, as did the terrible uncertainty of what I meant for her, if anything. She had shown a will anxiety for me to return, and it wasn't only to help her live through Marilena's illness. She had told me so while I was trying to console her:

"I'm too strong to need consolation, Stratis. I know what to do when Marilena dies."

165

At times she seemed to lean on me for protection; other moments even her breathing became sexual; then again she would stare vacantly into space without saying a word. And then, she might say something totally unrelated to her other actions:

"When we go back to Athens, I want to be able to see you. I want you to remain my friend."

And I the strong male, was unable to tell her that I didn't want to be her friend: I wanted to be her lover, to live with her like we had lived those two days on the island.

But I would settle for being her friend only. I wanted her so desperately ...

A month ago she had made me get on a boat without knowing where it was headed for. Now where would she lead me?

And yet I was unable to stay away from her.

When she left the restaurant where we were having dinner to buy pills for Marilena, I was in a frenzy until she returned. Stupid, childish thoughts went through my mind: and if she doesn't return, I wondered, what will I do?

She was driving me crazy, that was a fact. When she returned from the pharmacy, her first words were:

"Do you think we'll ever be able to be together again like we were those two days?"

Just like that, out of the blue. It was incredible how she had managed to wipe out all traces of logic in me. A word from her, and I was in heaven; a frown and I was miserable.

It could have been the perfect relationship, but instead it was sheer torture. And yet, even at times when I could only feel sorry for myself, I couldn't deny the truth: I wanted her beyond all reason, and as long as I didn't have her my mind was blown apart.

When we returned home that night, there was, of course, no hope we would make love. We were involved in a death procession and only if I were a necrophiliac could I have made love to her in that house.

She slept in my room, since Marilena had been moved to the single one. It had become round-the-clock torture: her breathing in the next bed was the most merciless company I could imagine. I would wake up - providing, that is, I was able to fall asleep - and get up to look at her. She was sleeping peacefully, her raven hair hiding half her face. Only when daylight broke was I able to fall into a deep, troubled sleep.

Often through the long, lonely night a deep, muffled moan would be heard from the next room, like the melody of death. The atmosphere in the house that was once full of joy had become unbearable macabre. I couldn't take it, but I knew that if I left Alexandra would be gone forever.

CHAPTER 27

The days that followed were exactly as the doctor had foreseen.

She no longer recognized us. Her sleep was full of nightmares often accompanied by piercing screams of terror and agony. She screamed because she was afraid of staying alone in a dark infinity; she was afraid that everyone was leaving her to remain there forever. It was the terror of someone who is facing the unknown solitude of death.

After the screams she would make tremendous efforts to breathe which sounded each time like a death rattle. It wasn't her agony at such times; it was the cursed desease spreading through her body and choking her lungs.

In just a few days, Alexandra had truly broken down. She was unable to cope with the approach of death. It was only natural, after all: it's not possible to imagine the end of life when you're only at the beginning.

Alexandra was fading away along with Marilena. She wouldn't eat a thing and was losing weight rapidly. She wouldn't budge from Marilena's side; she was obviously on the verge of a nervous breakdown. Now that Marilena no longer recognized us, it was impossible for Alexandra to compromise.

Marilena's young heart was still beating, but every other part of her had already died. There was no need for either

her or us to live through the agony of the last few days; she had turned into a lifeless body, the heart of which continued to beat in one of nature's caprices.

It wasn't long, however, before her heart followed the rest of her body into eternity. It was morning. The doctor was there, although his presence, too, was no longer necessary. Alexandra and I were sitting on the sofa when he came out of Marilena's room.

He came toward us and took both Alexandra's hands in his:

"It's over", he said. "She can rest now."

"What?" she screamed and started to run into the room.

I didn't let her. I took her into my arms where she remained, crying, until the doctor left. Then we went into the room together. Marilena was dead. The doctor had crossed her hands over her chest.

All the agony was gone from her face; she looked as if she were sleeping peacefully and would soon wake up to go to the beach.

Alexandra was standing behind me. I couldn't see what she was doing but I could hear her sobs. I covered Marilena's face with the sheet. The end of life is always a cruel sight.

I took Alexandra out of the house with me. She followed me silently as I went to telephone her mother.

"It is over?" she asked between sobs. "She wanted to die in Mykonos, near you, where she had the last pleasant memories in life."

Her words were a piercing stab on my conscience: the last pleasant memories in life! The way I had treated her, the memories could hardly have been pleasant!

And yet, she had wanted to stay with me. Perhaps she

was happy just to be in my company, whether it was sweet or bitter. The thought was somewhat comforting for my sinful conscience.

I told her mother that I would try to put the coffin on the boat arriving in Piraeus the next morning. Alexandra, unable to bear listening to this macabre conversation, was waiting for me outside. She was sitting on the steps and staring out at the sea through the tears in her eyes.

I took her to a cafeneion and went to see about the boat and the coffin. When I returned, she startled me:

"Did you get a ticket for me?"

"What do you want a ticket for?" I asked in astonishment.

"I simply asked you if you got one", she said in a bitter tone.

It wasn't the time for objections and advise. I just asked:

"No. Why?"

"I want to travel with Marilena tonight."

It would have been a sacrilege to object. Her tone made it obvious that she had made up her mind to go.

I went and purchased a ticket and gave it to her. I couldn't deny her the right to accompany her friend for the last time.

At midnight the coffin was loaded onto the launch which would take it to the boat. I looked on and remembered how we had come together two and a half months earlier. I felt the tears rolling down my face.

Then Alexandra got into the launch. She turned and looked at me:

"So long, Stratis" she said in a quiet voice.

"I'll wait for you to return. Come back soon". I answered in the same low voice.

She continued looking at me without saying a word until the launch disappeared into the darkness.

With a heavy load on my heart I started walking along the harbor, looking for somewhere to have a drink. I went into Bobby's little bar where only a few foreigners were having nightcaps. Bobby brought me a scotch and clinked his glass with mine. He didn't say anything, but the look on his face revealed understanding and sorrow.

Sipping slowly on the second scotch, I felt a tap on my back. It was Fouskis, who offered condolences and sat next to me. "What are you going to do now?" he asked.

"I'm waiting", I answered.

He didn't ask me what I was waiting for.

I left and headed for the house. I couldn't drink. The dead Marilena was more alive than ever in my mind. I thought, too, of Alexandra, alone and innocent to death, accompanying a coffin in the dark seas. It made me feel even more miserable. Perhaps I should have gone with her.

To this day I haven't been able to explain to myself why I hadn't gone along. It was a human enough reaction; deep down perhaps I still considered the dead girl responsible for my situation.

There would have been no place for me at the funeral procession in the sea. Alexandra shouldn't have gone either. The coffin would be picked up by her family. We had no place among them.

Suddenly I had become harsh and bitter; an erotic optimism told me I had made the right decision. I walked along the dark, silent streets, my guilty conscience chasing away the optimism. Maybe I should have gone: what if my hurried decision meant I would lose Alexandra forever?

I reached the house and opened the door. A strong

smell of cologne and vinegar was in the air: it was the cologne the village women had splashed on Marilena before dressing her and the bottle of vinegar which they traditionally break on the door before taking out a coffin.

My once happy household had suddenly been drenched in the smell of death. I opened all the windows to get in some air and then looked into Marilena's room. They had taken the matress out to be aired; a live human being would one day take the place of the dead girl. Life had stopped for one person but not for the rest of us.

I tried to get used to the idea - I didn't, after all, want to be buried alive in that house. I went out to the terrace and lay down on a chair, staring vacantly at the moon. Marilena had looked at that same moon, I thought. It was the last moon she had ever looked at ....

How strange that we are unable to become accustomed to the most common event in life: its end. As long as it doesn't in some way touch us, we never think of it - even though we know it's where we're all headed for. Every minute that goes by, every passing day, brings us closer to death. Yet, when the life of someone close to you ends, when you know you will never, but never, see a familiar face again, it's impossible to fathom. I couldn't really believe that Marilena would never, but never be around anymore.

The boat would be near Yaros now, but the raging seas wouldn't bother her motionless body in its wooden crate ...

"Which island is that, Don?" she had asked me when we were coming to Mykonos.

I followed the moon until it disappeared behind Delos. I looked at the thousands of stars in the sky. One of them would be Marilena's soul, looking down on us forever.

I remembered when I was a little boy and I had asked my mother what the stars were made of.

"They're the souls of people who are dead", she explained.

"When I die, my boy, and you look up at the stars, you'll know that one of them is your mother, taking care of you from up there."

CHAPTER 28

The next day I went down to the harbor. I didn't really expect Alexandra to return yet, since the funeral would be held in the afternoon.

Some fishermen came and had a couple of ouzos with me. In the afternoon I sat home and read. The weather had changed for good; the sun would occasionally peek out from behind the clouds and then disappear again. It was winter.

I woke up early the next morning. It was cold, but my spirits were high and light: today Alexandra would return.

At three I went down to wait for the boat. I had seen it approaching from my window, dipping in and out of the raging sea.

The first launch arrived and out of it came various people, none of which resembled Alexandra.

The second launch was only half full; no other would follow. I watched it approaching with hope that soon became disappointment. She wasn't there. When the last person got out all my hopes were dead.

With a heavy heart I walked to the other side of the harbor. She should have come back today, I thought, and tried to give myself an explanation for why she hadn't.

I was a psychological mess. Loneliness and the island's wintry gloom had gotten the better of me. The streets were empty, the shops no longer opened. From one day to the next, Mykonos had become a ghost town.

The children were in school. The white houses no longer sparkled; there was no sun, they weren't whitewashed in winter. The windows were hazy from the cold.

I walked along without a destination. The only emotion left in me was expectation, however slight. I looked around: everything seemed dead; even the sun was setting early on that cold, grey afternoon. I felt as if my life were setting with it, in the vast loneliness of a deserted island.

The few people who had arrived had gone hurriedly into their houses. There wasn't a soul on the harbor.

Only the statue of Manto stood proudly, looking over the island and out to the sea. The look on her marble face was almost inhuman, scornful of disappointment and sorrow. I looked at her to draw some strength; I had no hope left and the truth had made itself evident.

Her marble face sometimes became human; now she was looking at me with compassion, the one thing I needed most. Feeling miserable and deserted, I felt I would never smile again. What if I were alive? There was no life for me without her. Death had won over me.

Marilena had won Alexandra by dying. She never came back to me.